Catholic Readings and Prayer book for Advent

Daily Scriptures, Reflections, and Prayers to Prepare Your Heart for the Coming of Christ

Elizabeth Knowles

Table of Contents

Part IV: The Third Week of Advent – The Candle of Joy (Gaudete Sunday)

Part V: The Fourth Week of Advent – The Candle of Love

Part VI: The O Antiphons (December 17–23)

Part VII: The Coming of Christ – Christmas Eve and Christmas Day

Introduction

Welcome, dear friend in Christ, to the sacred season of Advent—a time of joyful waiting, quiet reflection, and spiritual renewal. Advent is not merely a countdown to Christmas; it is a profound journey of faith, hope, peace, joy, and love. It is the Church's beautiful invitation to slow down, quiet the noise of the world, and prepare our hearts for the coming of Jesus Christ—our Savior and Redeemer.

For centuries, the Catholic Church has set aside these four weeks before Christmas as a season of anticipation and prayerful longing. It is a time that echoes the ancient cry of the prophets: *"Prepare the way of the Lord!"* (Isaiah 40:3). In Advent, we remember the generations who waited for the promised Messiah, and we, too, wait—not just to celebrate His birth in Bethlehem, but to welcome Him anew into our hearts and to look forward to His glorious return.

Advent reminds us that God always keeps His promises. Even in darkness, there is light; even in longing, there is hope. It calls us to make room for Christ in the midst of our daily busyness, to refocus our attention from the noise of the season to the stillness of God's presence. As we light each candle on the Advent wreath and turn the pages of this prayerbook, may our hearts be filled with renewed wonder at the mystery of the Incarnation—God made flesh, dwelling among us.

How to Use This Prayerbook

This *Catholic Daily Readings and Prayerbook for Advent* is designed to be your faithful companion through this holy season. Each section follows the rhythm of the Church's Advent weeks—Hope, Peace, Joy, and Love—helping you enter deeply into the spiritual meaning of each candle on the Advent wreath.

Each day features a **Scripture Reading**, **Reflection**, and **Prayer**, thoughtfully crafted to guide your heart closer to Christ. You may use it individually, as a family, or in a parish group setting. Whether in the quiet of morning, during evening prayer, or before lighting the Advent wreath at home, these readings and prayers are meant to help you pause and dwell in the presence of God.

Take time with each reading. Let the Word of God speak to you personally. Reflect on the Scripture and ask: *What is God saying to me today?* Pray slowly and intentionally, inviting the Holy Spirit to illuminate your heart.

This prayerbook also includes **traditional Catholic prayers**, **hymns**, and **special devotions** such as the **O Antiphons**, which have been cherished by the Church for centuries. These ancient prayers, used from December 17 to 23, call upon Christ with titles drawn from Scripture—O Wisdom, O Lord, O Root of Jesse—and remind us of who He is and why He came.

Above all, use this book as a sacred space—a meeting place between your soul and the God who loves you infinitely. This is not a checklist of prayers to complete but a spiritual journey of love and transformation.

The Meaning and Symbols of Advent

Advent is rich with sacred symbols that speak to the heart and soul of the believer. Each element, from the purple vestments worn by priests to the evergreen wreaths adorning our homes, carries deep spiritual meaning.

The word *Advent* comes from the Latin *adventus*, meaning "coming." It celebrates three comings of Christ:

1. **His coming in history**, when He was born of the Virgin Mary in Bethlehem.
2. **His coming in mystery**, through grace and the Holy Eucharist into our hearts today.
3. **His coming in majesty**, at the end of time when He will return to judge the living and the dead.

The **color purple** used during Advent symbolizes penance and preparation, reminding us to turn our hearts back to God. Some parishes also use **blue or violet** hues to signify hope and expectation. The **evergreen wreath**, with its circle shape, symbolizes God's eternal love—without beginning or end. The **candles**, glowing brighter with each passing week, remind us that Christ is the Light of the World, dispelling the darkness of sin and fear.

Even the **shortness of daylight** in December becomes a sacred sign. As the world grows darker, the Church's light grows stronger. Each candle we light proclaims that the true Light is coming—and no darkness can overcome it.

The Advent wreath holds a place of honor in both churches and Catholic homes. Traditionally made of evergreen branches, it carries four candles—three purple and one rose—each representing a virtue and a week of Advent.

- **The First Candle (Purple): The Candle of Hope**
  It reminds us of the prophets, especially Isaiah, who foretold the coming of the Messiah. It calls us to trust in God's promises and to wait with expectant hearts.
- **The Second Candle (Purple): The Candle of Peace**
  It symbolizes Christ as the Prince of Peace. As we light it, we are invited to reconcile with God and others, finding serenity in His presence.
- **The Third Candle (Rose): The Candle of Joy (Gaudete Sunday)**
  Its rose color signals rejoicing, for the Lord is near. This week is a pause in our penance, a moment to celebrate the joyful hope of Christ's arrival.
- **The Fourth Candle (Purple): The Candle of Love**
  It reminds us of the boundless love of God revealed in the gift of His Son. Love is the flame that prepares our hearts for the birth of the Savior.

Finally, on **Christmas Eve or Christmas Day**, a **white candle**—often placed in the center—is lit. This is the **Christ Candle**, symbolizing the light of Jesus that has come into the world. Its pure white glow proclaims that the waiting is over: *Emmanuel—God with us—has come!*

Advent is not only about preparing our homes with decorations or gifts but preparing our **souls** for the dwelling of Christ. The Lord desires not just to be remembered in a manger but to be born anew in the humble stable of our hearts.

We prepare through **prayer**, which keeps us rooted in God's presence. We prepare through **repentance**, turning away from sin and reconciling with God through the Sacrament of Penance. We prepare through **acts of love and charity**, reaching out to the poor, the lonely, and the brokenhearted.

This season invites us to open our hearts to grace—to make room for Christ where perhaps the world has crowded Him out. The more space we create for Him, the more peace we will experience.

Let this Advent be different. Let it be sacred. Let it be filled with intentional prayer, silence, and gratitude. As you walk through these pages—day by day, prayer by prayer—may you discover that Advent is not simply about waiting for Christmas, but about living every moment in joyful expectation of the One who has already come and who will come again.

May this *Catholic Daily Readings and Prayerbook for Advent* lead you to a deeper encounter with Christ, the Light of the World. May your heart become His dwelling place, and may the hope, peace, joy, and love of this holy season remain with you always.

Come, Lord Jesus. Come quickly and dwell among us.
✦

Sunday: The Promise of a Savior

Scripture Reading:

"The people who walked in darkness have seen a great light; upon those who dwelt in the land of gloom, a light has shone."
— **Isaiah 9:2**

The first Sunday of Advent begins with the glow of a single flame — the **Candle of Hope**. Its gentle light pierces the darkness, just as the promises of God pierced through the centuries of waiting for a Savior. As we light this first candle, we recall that our faith is not built upon wishful thinking or temporary comfort, but upon the eternal promises of a faithful God who never forgets His people.

Since the fall of Adam and Eve, humanity has lived with an ache in the heart — a longing to be restored, healed, and made whole again. Sin had brought separation, but even in humanity's failure, God's mercy was at work. The story of salvation began not in the manger of Bethlehem, but in the Garden of Eden, where God first promised that the seed of the woman would crush the serpent's head (Genesis 3:15). From that moment, all creation began to wait. Every prophet, every psalm, every longing heart looked forward to the coming of the Messiah — the One who would redeem and renew the world.

The prophet Isaiah, whose words we hear often during Advent, spoke of this coming Savior with deep conviction: *"A shoot shall sprout from the stump of Jesse, and from his roots a bud shall blossom."* (Isaiah 11:1). These words carried hope into the hearts of a weary people. Israel, like a tree cut down, seemed lifeless and defeated — yet God promised that new life would spring forth from what appeared dead. The Messiah, born of the line of David, would bring justice, peace, and light to all nations.

Hope, in the Christian sense, is not a fragile wish; it is a confident trust. It is the sure belief that what God has promised, He will fulfill. Advent invites us to stand alongside the people of Israel — to remember that we, too, are waiting for the full revelation of God's kingdom. We await not only the memory of Christ's birth, but His return in glory. The Promise of a Savior is both a historical truth and a present reality, reminding us that no matter how dark the world seems, the light of Christ is always approaching.

As we begin this first week of Advent, the **Candle of Hope** challenges us to trust again — to believe that God is at work even in the silence, even when our hearts are tired or our prayers seem unanswered. The same God who fulfilled His promise to send a Savior is faithful to fulfill His promises to you.

Perhaps your heart carries its own kind of waiting: waiting for healing, for forgiveness, for reconciliation, for peace. Advent teaches us that waiting is not wasted time when it is filled with faith. Just as Mary waited with love and expectancy, we too can wait with hope, knowing that God's timing is perfect. The Promise of a Savior tells us that no darkness is permanent, no sin is too great, and no life is too far gone for redemption.

Hope begins when we turn our gaze toward the One who comes — Jesus Christ, the Light of the World. His coming is the ultimate fulfillment of God's love: not a distant dream, but a living reality that continues to transform hearts and lives.

As you meditate on this first Sunday of Advent, consider what it means for Christ to be your personal Savior. He came not just to the world in general, but for *you*. He entered into human weakness, pain, and struggle so that you might find in Him the strength to endure and the grace to begin again. His promise remains as true today as it was to the shepherds in Bethlehem: *"Behold, I bring you good news of great joy which will come to all people."* (Luke 2:10).

Let your heart rest in that good news. The Savior has come — and He is coming still. Every Advent season renews this truth: that God's promises never fail, and His mercy never ends. As you light your first candle and whisper your first prayer, may the warmth of hope take root within you. Let the small flame remind you that even one flicker of faith can light up the darkest night.

Reflection:

The Promise of a Savior invites us to trust in God's faithfulness even when we cannot see the outcome. It calls us to believe that His plan for humanity — and for each of us — unfolds in perfect love. Like the people of Israel, we may walk through seasons of silence, but God's Word assures us that *the dawn is coming.* Hope is born in every heart that dares to believe that God will do what He has said.

Prayer:

Heavenly Father,
On this first Sunday of Advent, we thank You for the promise of a Savior. We thank You for the hope that fills the world through Your Son, Jesus Christ. As we light the first candle, may its flame remind us that Your light always overcomes the darkness.

Help us to trust You more deeply this week — to wait with patience, to hope with confidence, and to rejoice in Your faithfulness. Let our hearts be filled with expectation and peace as we prepare for the coming of Christ. Renew our faith, O Lord, and teach us to see Your hand at work even in the smallest moments of our lives.

Come, Lord Jesus, our promised Redeemer.
Shine Your light into our hearts and make us ready for Your coming.
Amen.

Monday: Trusting God's Timing

Scripture Reading:

"For everything there is a season, and a time for every matter under heaven."
— **Ecclesiastes 3:1**

On this second day of our Advent journey, we are invited to pause and reflect on one of the most challenging yet beautiful aspects of faith — **trusting in God's perfect timing**.

Advent itself is a season of waiting. It teaches us that God's plans unfold not according to our impatience or expectations, but according to His divine wisdom and love. From the moment sin entered the world, God's people waited centuries for the Messiah. Prophets foretold His coming, generations passed the promise along, and countless hearts longed for the day when God would send His Redeemer. But that promise did not come overnight. It came in the fullness of time — when the world was ready, and when Mary's "yes" opened the door for salvation.

We, too, live in a world that resists waiting. We want answers immediately, blessings instantly, and miracles on demand. Yet God often works quietly and slowly, forming something beautiful in the silence of our waiting. He knows the perfect moment to act — and though His timing may not match ours, it is never late.

In the Scriptures, we see this truth repeated again and again. Abraham waited for the birth of Isaac. Joseph waited through years of hardship before seeing the purpose of his trials. The Israelites waited in exile for restoration. And Mary, full of grace, waited in faith for the fulfillment of the angel's promise. None of these waited in vain. Each learned that **hope is not passive**, but active trust — a steady belief that God is faithful, even when His plan is hidden from view.

Trusting in God's timing does not mean pretending that waiting is easy. There are moments when it feels like God is silent, or distant, or slow to respond. Yet in those moments, He is preparing something greater than we can imagine. Sometimes, the waiting itself becomes the place of transformation — where our faith deepens, our hearts are refined, and our souls learn to rest in His providence.

Consider this: if Christ had come sooner, perhaps the world would not have been ready. If He had come later, perhaps humanity's longing would have grown cold. God's plan unfolded at the exact moment that brought the greatest glory to Him and the greatest good to us. The same is true for every season of your life. The promise God has made to you will be fulfilled at the appointed time — not too early, not too late, but precisely when your heart is ready to receive it.

This Advent, let your waiting become an act of worship. Instead of asking, *"When, Lord?"*, begin to pray, *"What are You teaching me in this moment?"* The stillness of waiting is not emptiness; it is sacred ground where God is molding you into who He created you to be.

When we learn to trust God's timing, our hearts find peace. The world may rush ahead, but the soul that rests in divine timing walks in freedom. Hope becomes stronger, faith becomes deeper, and joy becomes steady. Remember: God is never in a hurry, but He is always on time.

Reflection:

Trusting in God's timing means surrendering our need for control and resting in His wisdom. The waiting heart is not forgotten — it is cherished and prepared. Just as the earth must rest before the seed sprouts, your spirit must sometimes wait before the promise blossoms. The first candle of Advent reminds us that God's promises are sure, even when they take time. Every moment of waiting is an opportunity to grow in trust and to say with quiet confidence: *"Your will be done, Lord."*

Prayer:

Heavenly Father,
You are the Lord of all time and seasons. You know the plans You have for me, and they are plans of goodness and hope. Yet in moments when I grow impatient or discouraged, remind me that Your timing is perfect and Your promises never fail.

Teach me to wait with faith. Help me to trust You in the silence, to listen for Your voice in the stillness, and to find peace in Your will. Like Mary, may I say "yes" to Your plan, even when I do not fully understand it.

Lord Jesus, as I walk through this first week of Advent, strengthen my hope. Let me rest in the assurance that You are working all things together for my good and for Your glory. When my heart wavers, whisper to my soul that You are near, and that in Your time, everything will be made beautiful.

Come, Lord Jesus, fill me with patient hope as I await Your coming.
Amen.

Tuesday: The Light of Hope

Scripture Reading:

"The light shines in the darkness, and the darkness has not overcome it."
— **John 1:5**

As the days of Advent unfold, the glow of the first candle continues to remind us that even the smallest light can chase away the deepest darkness. This is the light of hope — the light that began to flicker in the hearts of God's people long before the Savior was born. It is the same light that burns within us today, a radiant promise that no shadow is too great for God's grace to overcome.

The world into which Christ was born was one of spiritual darkness. Centuries of silence had passed since the prophets last spoke. Israel longed for deliverance, and many wondered if God had forgotten His people. But in that stillness, in that sacred waiting, a light began to rise — not from earthly power, but from divine mercy. Into the quiet night of Bethlehem, the Light of the World stepped forth.

That same light, born in a humble manger, now shines in every heart that believes. Advent calls us to rekindle that flame — to let the light of Christ grow brighter within us day by day. Just as dawn slowly breaks through the horizon, the light of hope gently fills the soul that turns toward God in faith.

We live in a world that often feels shadowed by fear, uncertainty, and pain. Wars rage, hearts grow weary, and faith is tested. Yet the message of Advent is clear: **the darkness does not win**. God's light cannot be extinguished. Every act of kindness, every prayer whispered in faith, every moment of love shared — these are rays of that same divine light shining in the world today.

Hope, like a candle, must be protected and nourished. It flickers when the winds of doubt or disappointment blow, but it endures when we shield it with prayer and faith. Just as a small flame can light an entire room, your faith — no matter how small — can bring warmth and guidance to those around you. When you let the light of Christ shine through your words and actions, you become a beacon of hope for others who may still be lost in the shadows.

The beauty of Advent is that it does not deny the existence of darkness. It simply declares that light is stronger. Even a single flame has power to break the night. In the same way, Christ's presence in your heart has power to illuminate the deepest places of fear, sorrow, or doubt. Each day you choose to trust Him, the light grows brighter. Each time you turn to prayer, the flame strengthens.

Let this day remind you that hope is not a distant dream but a living light within you. The same Spirit that hovered over the waters at creation, the same power that guided Israel by a pillar of fire, and the same radiance that shone from the angels on that first Christmas night — that same divine light dwells in you. You carry the promise of God wherever you go.

So if today feels heavy, if you are facing uncertainty or grief, lift your eyes to the flame of the Advent candle and remember: Christ has come, and He will come again. The light has already entered the world. The darkness may whisper, but it cannot conquer. Hope lives because Jesus lives.

Reflection:

Every candle we light during Advent is a symbol of God's presence drawing nearer. The first candle burns with hope — not the shallow hope of wishful thinking, but the confident assurance that Christ is faithful to His word. This light reminds us that no matter how long the night, morning always comes. As disciples of Christ, we are called to reflect that light in our families, workplaces, and communities. The more we allow His light to shine through us, the more the world will see that God's promises are true.

Take a moment today to sit in silence before the flame of the candle or the cross on your wall. Watch the light dance gently, and let it become a prayer: a silent offering of trust that God is with you, even in your waiting.

Prayer:

O Radiant Lord,
You are the Light that pierces every darkness, the Flame that never fades. As I journey through this week of hope, let Your light shine in my heart and drive away all fear, doubt, and despair.

When I am tempted to give in to discouragement, remind me that Your presence is my strength. When the world seems lost in shadow, make me a bearer of Your light — gentle, steady, and faithful. Help me to bring warmth to those who are cold, comfort to those who mourn, and hope to those who have forgotten how to believe.

Lord Jesus, Light of the World, shine in me and through me. Kindle in my heart a flame that will never go out — a flame of hope that leads others to You.
Come and illumine my path, that I may walk in Your truth and live in the joy of Your promise.

Amen.

Wednesday: The Prophets Speak

Scripture Reading:

"A voice cries out: 'In the wilderness prepare the way of the Lord, make straight in the desert a highway for our God.'"
— **Isaiah 40:3**

As the first week of Advent unfolds, the light of the **Candle of Hope** glows brighter, reminding us that God's promises are not forgotten. Today, we listen to the powerful voices of the prophets—men chosen by God to prepare His people for the coming of the Messiah. Their words echo across centuries, carrying messages of warning, repentance, faith, and above all, **hope**.

The prophets were God's messengers in dark times. They lived among people who had strayed far from His covenant—people weary from war, exile, and silence. Yet, through these prophets, God continued to speak, assuring His children that even in their suffering, He had not abandoned them. Theirs was not a message of despair but of restoration; not of punishment, but of promise.

Among them, **Isaiah** stands as one of the greatest heralds of hope. He saw beyond the brokenness of his time and proclaimed the coming of a child who would change the world: *"For unto us a child is born, unto us a son is given; and the government will be upon his shoulder; and his name shall be called Wonderful Counselor, Mighty God, Everlasting Father, Prince of Peace."* (Isaiah 9:6).

Through Isaiah's prophecy, we glimpse the heart of Advent — God's plan unfolding through human history, step by step, until the fullness of time. Isaiah foretold not only the birth of the Savior but also His mission: to heal the brokenhearted, proclaim liberty to captives, and bring light to those who dwell in darkness. (Isaiah 61:1).

Then came **Jeremiah**, the prophet of a new covenant. Amid exile and sorrow, he spoke words of unimaginable comfort: *"The days are coming, says the Lord, when I will make a new covenant with the house of Israel... I will place my law within them, and write it upon their hearts."* (Jeremiah 31:31,33). His message revealed that God's ultimate desire was not just to lead His people externally, but to dwell within them — a promise fulfilled in Christ, the Word made flesh.

And we must not forget **John the Baptist**, the last and greatest of the prophets, whose voice cried out in the wilderness. John prepared the way of the Lord not only through his preaching but through his entire life of humility and repentance. His call still resounds: *"Repent, for the kingdom of heaven is at hand."* (Matthew 3:2). He stands as the bridge between the Old Covenant and the New, pointing us directly to the Lamb of God who takes away the sins of the world.

Each prophet, in his own way, proclaimed one central truth: **God keeps His promises**. Though His people wandered, He remained steadfast. Though centuries passed, His plan never faltered. Their words are living reminders that hope is not born of circumstance but of God's unchanging faithfulness.

During Advent, we are called to become like the prophets — to prepare the way of the Lord in our own hearts and in the world around us. Their voices urge us to turn away from distraction, sin, and fear, and to make room for Christ. Just as they spoke light into darkness, we too are invited to speak words of faith, encouragement, and peace into our families, communities, and workplaces.

When we proclaim hope, we participate in the same mission as Isaiah, Jeremiah, and John. The world today still longs for good news — and that news remains the same: *the Savior is coming.*

Let us open our hearts to the prophetic voice of God that still whispers to us through Scripture, prayer, and the stillness of Advent. The prophets remind us that even when we cannot see the full picture, God is working. Even when the night feels long, dawn is near.

Reflection:

The prophets did not speak only for their time — they speak to ours as well. Their words are living truth, reminding us that God's promises span generations. Every prophecy fulfilled in Christ assures us that every word He has spoken to us will also come true.

In a world that often mocks faith and doubts divine timing, the prophets encourage us to remain steadfast. Their voices teach us that faith is not blind optimism, but trusting God even when the outcome is unseen. They teach us that every valley will be raised, every mountain made low, and that the glory of the Lord will indeed be revealed. (Isaiah 40:4–5).

Ask yourself today: *What "valleys" in my heart need to be lifted up? What "mountains" of pride or fear need to be leveled so that Christ may enter freely?* As we listen to the prophets, may we respond not with fear, but with faith — not with anxiety, but with hope.

Prayer:

God of the Prophets,
You spoke through holy men and women to prepare the world for Your coming. Through their words, You gave Your people courage to wait and faith to believe. As I meditate on their message today, open my heart to hear Your voice anew.

Teach me to trust Your promises even when the waiting feels long. Give me the courage of Isaiah to proclaim Your truth, the patience of Jeremiah to believe in Your covenant, and the humility of John the Baptist to point others toward You.

Lord, may I be a bearer of Your hope in the world. Let my words, like the prophets', prepare the way for Your coming — in my heart, in my family, and in all who long for Your light.

Come, Lord Jesus, and fulfill once more the promise spoken through the prophets:

that You would dwell among us, and that every heart may see Your glory.

Amen.

Thursday: Faith in the Waiting

Scripture Reading:

"The Lord is good to those who wait for Him, to the soul that seeks Him."
— **Lamentations 3:25**

The story of Advent is a story of waiting — not restless waiting, but **faithful waiting**. It is the sacred space between God's promise and its fulfillment, between what is spoken and what is seen. The people of Israel waited generation after generation for the coming of the Messiah. And even now, we wait for His glorious return. Waiting, then, is not wasted time for the Christian; it is holy time — a time of trust, surrender, and preparation.

We live in an age where waiting seems like an inconvenience. Everything moves fast: news, messages, food, and plans. We grow frustrated when things do not happen instantly. Yet, in God's economy, waiting is often where the most important transformation happens. It is in the waiting that faith deepens. It is in the waiting that patience matures. It is in the waiting that we learn to lean not on our own understanding, but on the unchanging faithfulness of God.

The prophets waited. Mary waited. Joseph waited. Even the heavens seemed to hold their breath before the birth of the Savior. Every promise in Scripture — from Abraham's covenant to the angel's announcement — carried with it a period of waiting. And through it all, God was working quietly, weaving together His perfect plan.

Faith in the waiting does not mean we sit idly by. It means we keep praying even when answers seem far away. It means we keep believing even when we feel uncertain. It means we trust that God is working behind the scenes, arranging details that we cannot yet see.

Imagine the people of Israel during the long centuries between the prophets and the coming of Christ. Many must have wondered if God had grown silent. Yet the silence was not absence; it was preparation. God was setting the stage for the greatest act of love the world would ever know. When the fullness of time had come, He sent His Son — not a moment too soon, not a second too late.

Our lives, too, are filled with seasons of waiting. Perhaps you are waiting for healing, for reconciliation, for a breakthrough, for peace. The first week of Advent invites you to bring all those longings before God and to rest in His promise: *"The Lord is good to those who wait for Him."* He never forgets His children. He never abandons His Word. The same faithfulness that brought Christ into the world is the faithfulness that will sustain you now.

Waiting in faith means holding onto hope even when circumstances seem dark. It is choosing to believe that the seed God planted in your heart will bloom in its season. Just as the earth must endure the stillness of winter before the blossoms of spring, your soul must sometimes sit quietly before the warmth of His promise breaks forth.

The Advent season is God's gentle reminder that the waiting is not the end of the story — it is the threshold of a miracle. Each day we light the candle of hope, its flame burns a little higher, a little stronger, a little closer to the light of Christmas. And so it is with our faith. The more we trust in Him during the waiting, the brighter our hope becomes.

Reflection:

Faith in the waiting is an act of surrender. It requires us to loosen our grip on our own plans and rest in the assurance that God's timing is perfect. Waiting stretches our trust and purifies our desires until they align with His will.

In those moments when you are tempted to despair, remember that the same God who fulfilled His promise to send a Savior is the same God working in your life today. The waiting is not a delay — it is a divine pause filled with purpose.

Ask yourself: *What is God teaching me in this season of waiting? Where might He be strengthening my faith, deepening my patience, or preparing my heart for something greater?*

The waiting is holy ground. Walk through it with faith.

Prayer:

Faithful and Loving Father,
You are the God of every season — the One who speaks,

the One who fulfills, and the One who sustains us in between. Thank You for reminding me through Advent that waiting is not wasted time but a time of grace.

When I grow impatient, calm my heart. When doubt creeps in, remind me of Your promises. When I cannot see Your hand, help me to trust Your heart. Teach me to wait with faith, to believe with hope, and to love with steadfast devotion.

Lord Jesus, as I journey through this week of hope, strengthen my faith in Your timing. Like Mary, may I learn to wait with trust and humility, believing that Your promises will never fail.

Come, Lord Jesus, into my waiting — and turn it into worship.
Amen.

Would you like me to continue with **Friday: Strength in His Word** next? It will explore how Scripture sustains our hope and faith as we continue the Advent journey.

Friday: Strength in His Word

Scripture Reading:

"Your word is a lamp to my feet and a light to my path."
— **Psalm 119:105**

By the time we reach Friday of the first week of Advent, the flame of the **Candle of Hope** has burned for several days—its light steady and faithful. It reminds us that even when the world grows dark, God's Word continues to guide and strengthen those who seek Him.

The journey of faith can often feel uncertain. We may not see the full picture of what God is doing, and our hearts may waver between trust and fear. Yet in these moments, Scripture becomes our compass, our nourishment, and our strength. Through His Word, God speaks—not only to nations and prophets, but to every individual heart willing to listen.

From the beginning of time, God's Word has been life-giving. *"Let there be light,"* He said, and creation was born. His Word carried the power to form the stars, calm the seas, and bring dry bones back to life. That same Word became flesh and dwelt among us in the person of Jesus

Christ. Every promise in Scripture finds its fulfillment in Him.

During Advent, we are invited to rediscover the strength found in God's Word. It is not a collection of ancient sayings, but a living voice that still breathes hope into weary souls. Every verse of Scripture carries divine power to renew, heal, and transform. When we open the Bible, we do not merely read about God—we encounter Him.

Think of the countless generations who clung to God's Word before the coming of the Savior. The people of Israel read the prophecies of Isaiah and Jeremiah, holding on to each promise as a lifeline in times of exile and despair. Even when all seemed lost, they found strength in His Word. It was their anchor, their light in the darkness. And when the time was right, that Word—long promised— became flesh in Bethlehem.

So it is with us today. When life feels uncertain, when our hearts grow heavy, God's Word steadies us. It reminds us who He is: faithful, merciful, and near. It reminds us who we are: beloved children, chosen to walk in His light. The more we feed upon Scripture, the stronger our faith becomes. His Word strengthens our hope and teaches us to see beyond our present struggles.

Many saints throughout history found strength in this truth. St. Jerome famously said, *"Ignorance of Scripture is ignorance of Christ."* The Word of God is not meant to sit closed on a shelf—it is meant to be lived. In it we find our guidance, our correction, our comfort, and our courage. Each passage read with a heart of prayer becomes a lamp that lights the path ahead.

As you move deeper into Advent, make time each day to read and meditate on the Scriptures. Even a single verse can become a prayer that carries you through the day. Read slowly. Listen attentively. Let the words take root in your heart. You will find that they bring not only knowledge, but peace.

In the noise of the modern world, God's voice is still clear and gentle for those who take time to listen. When everything around you feels uncertain, cling to His Word as your anchor. It is the same Word that guided prophets and apostles, saints and martyrs. It has not lost its power.

Let this be your confidence: that when you open the Scriptures, you are not merely reading about hope—you are meeting Hope Himself. Christ, the living Word, walks beside you. His words are spirit and life; they renew strength to the weary and courage to the fainthearted.

Reflection:

God's Word is alive. It does not grow old or fade with time. Every page reveals a facet of His heart, every verse carries a promise, and every command leads us toward freedom.

If your heart feels weary this Advent, open your Bible and ask the Holy Spirit to speak to you. Let His words enter your soul like light through a window. As the Psalmist said, *"The entrance of Your words gives light; it gives understanding to the simple."* (Psalm 119:130).

In the Word, we find both strength and direction. We find the courage to wait, the wisdom to discern, and the faith to keep walking when the road feels long.

Ask yourself: *Am I letting God's Word shape my days? Do I take time to listen for His voice in Scripture?* Let this Advent be a season of rediscovering the strength that comes from His Word.

Prayer:

Eternal Word of God,
Your voice has spoken through the ages, guiding Your people through times of joy and trial. Thank You for giving me the gift of Your Word—a lamp for my feet and a light for my path.

When I feel weak, let Your Word strengthen me. When I feel lost, let it guide me. When I am afraid, let it remind me that You are near. Help me to hunger for Your truth and to build my life upon the promises of Scripture.

Lord Jesus, You are the Word made flesh. Speak to my heart today and fill me with the peace that only Your presence can bring. May Your Word dwell richly in me, shaping my thoughts, my actions, and my prayers.

Come, Lord Jesus, speak anew through the pages of Your Word.
Let Your truth be my strength and Your promises my hope.
Amen.

Saturday: Preparing the Way

Scripture Reading:

"Prepare the way of the Lord, make straight His paths. Every valley shall be filled and every mountain and hill shall be made low; the crooked shall be made straight and the rough ways made smooth; and all flesh shall see the salvation of God."
— **Luke 3:4–6**

As we come to the close of the **First Week of Advent**, the single candle of hope burns more steadily, calling us to action — to prepare the way for the Lord. This is not a passive hope that merely waits; it is an active, living hope that transforms the heart and readies it for the coming of Christ.

John the Baptist's voice still echoes across the centuries: *"Prepare the way of the Lord!"* His cry was more than a call to repentance; it was an invitation to renewal. Through his words, God speaks to us even now, urging us to clear away whatever hinders our union with Him. Advent is that sacred time when we look within and ask: *Is my heart ready to receive Christ?*

The people of John's time were yearning for deliverance, yet many had grown spiritually dull. Their faith had become routine, and their hearts cluttered with worldly cares. In much the same way, we can allow the noise of daily life — the rush, the worries, the distractions — to crowd out the still, small voice of God. Advent calls us to pause, to make room again for the One who desires to dwell within us.

Preparing the way for the Lord begins with repentance — a sincere turning back to God. It means allowing the Holy Spirit to smooth out the rough places of pride, to lower the mountains of self-reliance, and to fill the valleys of fear and despair with His mercy. It is a gentle, ongoing conversion of the heart.

But preparation also means **hopeful expectation**. We do not prepare as people burdened with guilt or fear, but as children awaiting the arrival of Someone we love. Just as a home is cleaned and decorated before the arrival of a cherished guest, so too must our hearts be adorned with faith, love, and peace for the coming of our Savior.

In every act of kindness, every prayer whispered in faith, and every moment of forgiveness offered to others, we prepare a way for Christ to enter — not only into our own hearts but into the world around us. Every time we choose patience over anger, humility over pride, compassion over judgment, we are clearing a path for His light to shine.

Advent teaches us that preparing for Christ is not a one-time act but a lifelong posture. It is an attitude of the heart — always ready, always open, always waiting with joyful hope. Each day, the Lord comes to us in small, often unnoticed ways: through the face of the poor, the kindness of a friend, the quiet whisper in prayer. To prepare the way is to live with awareness that Emmanuel — *God with us* — is near.

We are called to be like candles in the dark world — simple, steady lights that point to the coming dawn. Our preparation is not meant to be heavy or burdensome, but peaceful and intentional. As we prepare, we discover that Christ has already been preparing a place for us — not only in heaven, but in the peace He plants within our souls.

This final reflection of the week reminds us that **hope leads to readiness**. True hope doesn't sit still; it moves us to live differently, to love more deeply, to forgive more freely. Hope transforms the waiting into worship.

As you conclude this first week of Advent, take a moment to examine your heart. What paths need to be straightened? What valleys need to be filled with faith? What mountains need to be brought low in humility? Let the Lord begin His work within you, and you will find that every step of preparation draws you closer to His peace.

Reflection:

Preparing the way of the Lord means creating room for grace. It means being attentive to His voice and ready to respond when He calls. The more we surrender to His will, the more He fills us with the light of His presence.

Ask yourself today: *How am I preparing for Christ's coming — not only at Christmas, but in my daily life?* Are there areas where I have resisted change or closed my heart to God's quiet invitations? Advent is the time to return, to begin again, to walk the straight path of faith, hope, and love.

Every act of repentance and renewal becomes a stone laid upon the road that leads to Bethlehem. As you prepare the way, know that Christ Himself is walking toward you with arms open wide.

Prayer:

Lord God,
You sent John the Baptist to prepare the hearts of Your people for the coming of the Savior. In this holy season of Advent, prepare my heart as well. Smooth the rough places within me, and fill the empty valleys of my soul with Your peace and grace.

Help me to turn away from anything that keeps me from You, and to open my life completely to Your presence. Teach me to wait with joy and to act with love, so that my words and deeds may reflect the light of Your Son.

As I end this first week of Advent, I place all my hopes in You. May the flame of this candle burn brightly in my heart, lighting the path of faith before me. Renew in me the courage to live as Your disciple — ready, willing, and filled with hope.

Come, Lord Jesus, prepare in me a home where You may dwell forever.
Amen.

Sunday: Peace in the Promise of Christ

Scripture Reading:

"Peace I leave with you; My peace I give to you. I do not give to you as the world gives. Do not let your hearts be troubled, and do not be afraid."
— **John 14:27**

A new candle glows on the Advent wreath this Sunday — the **Candle of Peace**. Its steady flame joins the first candle of hope, reminding us that true peace flows from hope fulfilled in Christ. The soft light whispers a message that every restless heart longs to hear: *Peace be with you.*

As we enter the second week of Advent, the theme shifts from hopeful waiting to the deep assurance of peace — not the fragile calm that the world offers, but the lasting peace that only Christ, the Prince of Peace, can give. This peace is not the absence of trouble, but the presence of God within every trial. It is the stillness that anchors the soul even when storms rage around us.

The promise of peace has always been at the heart of God's plan for His people. Through the prophets, He promised a Redeemer who would bring reconciliation — peace between God and humanity, peace among nations, and peace within every heart. Isaiah foresaw this when he proclaimed, *"The wolf shall dwell with the lamb... and a little child shall lead them."* (Isaiah 11:6). That peace — unimaginable and divine — came to us in the fragile form of a child in a manger.

When Jesus entered the world, the angels declared, *"Glory to God in the highest, and on earth peace to those on whom His favor rests."* (Luke 2:14). That heavenly announcement was more than a joyful proclamation; it was a declaration that the long-awaited promise had come true. Peace was no longer a distant hope — it was here, embodied in Christ Himself.

This peace is what Advent calls us to rediscover. It is not found in possessions, accomplishments, or fleeting comfort. It is found in surrender — in trusting that God holds every detail of our lives in His loving hands. The same Christ who calmed the waves with a single command still speaks to the storms within our hearts: *"Peace, be still."*

And yet, peace does not come automatically. It is a grace we must welcome and nurture. Often, the things that rob us of peace are not the great tragedies of life, but the small anxieties that creep in day by day — worry, fear, impatience, or the endless noise of the world around us. Advent offers a sacred pause — a time to silence the chaos and listen for God's voice once more.

To experience Christ's peace, we must first make room for it. Just as Mary prepared her heart to receive the Savior, we too must prepare our souls through prayer, confession, and forgiveness. Peace cannot dwell in a heart filled with resentment or distraction. It grows where humility, gratitude, and trust take root.

Christ's peace does not mean that life's difficulties vanish; rather, it means that we no longer face them alone. When we carry His peace within us, we carry something unshakeable — a light that no darkness can extinguish. Even when we walk through uncertainty, His peace sustains us. It flows from the assurance that God is with us, that His promises are true, and that His love will never fail.

Reflection:

The world promises peace through control, success, or comfort — but these forms of peace are temporary and fragile. The peace of Christ, on the other hand, is eternal. It transcends understanding, as St. Paul reminds us: *"And the peace of God, which surpasses all understanding, will guard your hearts and your minds in Christ Jesus."* (Philippians 4:7).

To live in that peace, we must surrender the illusion of control. We must trust that God's plan — though mysterious — is good. Advent peace comes when we let go of fear and embrace faith, when we choose forgiveness over anger, prayer over worry, and love over pride.

Today, as you light the second candle, take a moment to breathe deeply and rest in God's presence. Let the flickering flame remind you that peace begins not in the world, but within the heart that welcomes Christ.

Ask yourself: *Is there an area of my life where I have not allowed God's peace to enter? What would it look like to trust Him completely in that space?*

Invite the Prince of Peace to dwell there — and He will.

Prayer:

Prince of Peace,
You came into a troubled world to bring the calm of heaven to every restless heart. As I light the second candle of Advent, I ask You to fill me with Your peace — not as the world gives, but as only You can give.

Quiet my heart, Lord, where there is worry. Heal my spirit, where there is unrest. Teach me to trust You in every situation, knowing that Your plan is perfect and Your love is unchanging.

Help me to be an instrument of Your peace in my home, my work, and my community. Where there is division, let me sow unity; where there is sorrow, bring comfort; where there is darkness, shine Your light.

Lord Jesus, may Your peace reign in my heart and flow through me to others. As I journey through this week of Advent, remind me that You are near — and in Your presence, all fear is silenced.

Come, Prince of Peace, dwell within me and make my heart Your home.
Amen.

Monday: Peace in God's Presence

Scripture Reading:

"Be still, and know that I am God."
— **Psalm 46:10**

The second candle glows softly now — a gentle light reminding us of God's peace, a peace that flows not from outward calm, but from **His abiding presence**. Advent invites us to draw near to that stillness, to step away from the noise of the world and find rest in the God who never leaves us.

We live in a hurried age — one filled with constant motion, endless to-do lists, and voices competing for our attention. Yet, amid all this noise, God's voice remains soft and still, waiting for a heart that will stop long enough to listen. *"Be still,"* He says. In that stillness, peace is born.

The peace of God is not merely the absence of conflict; it is the assurance of His presence even in the midst of life's chaos. The same God who calmed the storm on the Sea of Galilee also whispers peace into the storms of our souls. He does not always take away our troubles, but He promises to be with us through them — and in His presence, our hearts find rest.

During Advent, we prepare for the coming of Christ not only by outward observance but by cultivating inner quiet — a spiritual stillness that allows us to hear the Lord speak. In the silence of prayer, in the gentle reading of Scripture, in the quiet glow of a candle, God meets us. He reminds us that peace is not something we achieve, but something we receive.

Consider the example of the Blessed Virgin Mary. When the angel announced God's plan for her life, she was not frantic or afraid; she received His word with trust. Her peace came not from understanding every detail but from knowing that **God was with her**. Her "yes" was rooted in faith, and her faith gave birth to peace.

So often, we lose peace because we forget that God's presence is constant. We may think He is far away, when in truth, He is closer than our next breath. In every moment — in joy and in sorrow, in work and in rest — He is there, quietly holding us in His love. When we turn our attention to Him, even briefly, the heart begins to settle, and a calm unlike any other fills our soul.

True peace comes when we surrender control and rest in God's hands. It does not depend on everything being perfect, but on our willingness to trust the One who is perfect. When we release our worries to Him in prayer, He fills the empty space with His presence. That is why St. Paul could write, *"Do not be anxious about anything, but in everything by prayer and supplication with thanksgiving let your requests be made known to God. And the peace of*

God… will guard your hearts and your minds in Christ Jesus." (Philippians 4:6–7).

When our hearts grow anxious, God's presence becomes our refuge. When we are overwhelmed, His Spirit breathes peace into us again. That peace doesn't always change our situation — but it always changes **us**.

The Advent season, therefore, is not just a countdown to Christmas — it is an invitation to dwell in peace right now. It is a time to slow down, to breathe deeply, and to be aware of Emmanuel, *God with us.* If we listen closely in prayer, we can hear Him saying: "I am here. I have never left you. Rest in Me."

So let today be a quiet day. Light your candle. Sit for a few moments in silence. Let the worries fade into the background and focus on the simple truth that God is present. In that stillness, His peace will meet you — gentle, steady, and everlasting.

Reflection:

Peace in God's presence is not found in escaping the world, but in inviting God into it. When we acknowledge Him in every part of our day — in the morning's quiet, in the work's noise, in the evening's rest — we discover that peace does not depend on circumstance but on connection.

Take time today to dwell in His presence. Speak less, listen more. Breathe deeply and remember: the same Lord who walked with Mary and Joseph walks with you. His peace is not distant — it is alive within you through His Spirit.

Ask yourself: *Do I make time each day to rest in God's presence? Do I turn to prayer when my peace feels lost, or do I try to carry the weight alone?*

Let this be a reminder that the One who calmed the winds and waves is the same One who can calm your soul.

Prayer:

Loving Father,
You are my refuge and my peace. In the stillness of this moment, I draw near to You. Calm the storms within me, and fill my heart with the quiet confidence that comes from Your presence.

Teach me to rest in You, to trust You completely, and to find my peace not in what the world offers, but in the assurance that You are always with me. When my mind is restless and my heart anxious, whisper to me, "Be still, and know that I am God."

Lord Jesus, Prince of Peace, make Your dwelling in my heart. Let Your presence guide my thoughts, rule my actions, and fill my days with serenity. May I carry Your peace into every conversation, every task, and every place I go today.

Come, Lord Jesus — be my peace, now and always.
Amen.

Tuesday: Listening to the Prophets

Scripture Reading:

"And the Lord God will do nothing, but He revealeth His secret unto His servants the prophets."
— **Amos 3:7**

The season of Advent is built upon the foundation of divine promises — and those promises were first proclaimed by the prophets. They were God's chosen messengers, voices crying out in a darkened world, calling the people to repentance and hope. Yet the message of the prophets was not only for Israel long ago; it is for us today. To find peace in our waiting, we must learn, once again, to **listen** to those voices that speak the truth of God.

In the Scriptures, the prophets were men and women who listened deeply to the Lord before they ever spoke. They spent time in His presence, carrying His Word in their hearts like a burning fire. They were not popular, nor did they speak what people wanted to hear; they spoke what they needed to hear. Their purpose was not to predict the future alone, but to reveal God's faithfulness and to call His people back to right relationship with Him.

During Advent, the prophets remind us that God's peace is not achieved through power or possessions, but through obedience and faith. Isaiah proclaims, *"If only you had paid attention to my commands, your peace would have been like a river."* (Isaiah 48:18). The peace God promises flows freely when our hearts are aligned with His Word. Listening to the prophets means listening for God's voice amid all the other noise — the noise of fear, pride, and distraction that fills our days.

The words of Isaiah, Jeremiah, Micah, and Malachi continue to echo through time. Each one announced the coming of the Messiah — the One who would bring peace not just to Israel, but to all nations. Micah foretold that He would be born in Bethlehem: *"But you, Bethlehem Ephrathah… out of you will come for me one who will be ruler over Israel."* (Micah 5:2). Isaiah spoke of Him as the Prince of Peace. Jeremiah called Him the Righteous Branch. And Malachi promised that the Sun of Righteousness would rise with healing in His wings.

These prophetic words, spoken centuries before Christ's birth, remind us that God's plan was never uncertain. Even in the silence between prophecy and fulfillment, He was working. Every word He spoke through the prophets was fulfilled perfectly in Jesus Christ. And that same God still speaks to us today — through Scripture, through prayer, and through the quiet movements of the Holy Spirit in our hearts.

But to hear Him, we must slow down. The voice of God is rarely loud or demanding; it comes as a whisper, gentle but firm. Advent invites us to cultivate that listening heart — the kind of heart that is not filled with noise but with longing, not with anxiety but with attention. Like the prophets, we must listen before we speak, pray before we act, and seek before we decide.

There is deep peace in listening to God. When we listen, we stop striving. When we listen, we stop trying to fix everything on our own. When we listen, we make room for His Word to direct our steps. The prophets found their strength in hearing God's voice — and so will we.

Listening to the prophets also calls us to **obedience**. Peace does not come merely from hearing, but from responding. The prophet Samuel learned this truth when he said, *"Speak, Lord, for Your servant is listening."* (1 Samuel 3:10). When we approach God's Word with the same openness, His voice brings order to our confusion and calm to our hearts.

This Advent, let us renew our commitment to listen attentively to the Word of God. The prophets' message was clear then, and it remains clear now: repent, return, and rejoice, for the Lord is near.

When you light your candle today, remember that peace is born in the listening heart — the heart that welcomes God's truth and allows it to take root. Just as the prophets' voices prepared the world for Christ's first coming, our obedience prepares our hearts for His coming anew.

Reflection:

Listening is one of the purest forms of prayer. It is in listening that we discover God's will and receive His peace. Yet so often, our prayer is filled only with words — our requests, our concerns, our plans. What if this Advent, we made space to simply *listen*?

The Lord still speaks through His Word, through the Church, through the quiet of our souls. If we listen carefully, we will find that He has been speaking all along — reminding us of His promises, urging us to forgiveness, guiding us toward holiness.

Ask yourself today: *Do I make time to listen to God's voice each day? Do I seek His direction before I make decisions, or only after?*

Peace flows from the heart that listens. As the prophets once did, let us listen well, and then walk faithfully in the path God sets before us.

Prayer:

Faithful Lord,
You spoke through Your prophets long ago, preparing the world for the coming of Your Son. Today, You continue to speak through Scripture, through Your Church, and through the gentle prompting of the Holy Spirit. Teach me to listen with a humble heart.

Still my mind, O Lord, so I may hear Your voice above the clamor of this world. Let Your Word take root in me, bringing peace where there is confusion, and strength where there is weakness.

Like Isaiah, may I proclaim Your goodness. Like Jeremiah, may I trust Your plans. Like John the Baptist, may I prepare the way for Your coming through the witness of my life.

Lord Jesus, Word made flesh, speak to me and dwell within me. May Your peace guard my heart and guide my steps today and always.

Come, Lord Jesus, speak to Your servant who is listening. **Amen.**

Wednesday: Preparing Our Hearts for Christ's Coming

Scripture Reading:

"In those days John the Baptist came, preaching in the wilderness of Judea and saying, 'Repent, for the kingdom of heaven has come near.'"
— **Matthew 3:1–2**

As the second week of Advent continues, the light of the **Candle of Peace** grows brighter. It shines as a gentle reminder that peace does not simply arrive when life becomes easy; it is born in the heart that has been made ready for Christ. Just as John the Baptist prepared the way for the Lord, we too must prepare our hearts for His coming.

The call to prepare is central to Advent. It is not about decorating homes, organizing gifts, or planning celebrations — though those things have their place. It is about preparing the **soul** — clearing the clutter, healing what has been broken, and making room for the Savior to dwell within us. Advent is an interior journey before it becomes an outward celebration.

When John the Baptist cried out in the wilderness, *"Prepare the way of the Lord!"* his words echoed the ancient prophecies of Isaiah. He called the people to repentance — not out of fear, but out of hope. Repentance, at its heart, is not simply feeling sorrow for sin; it is turning back to God with renewed love and faith. It is the act of sweeping away the dust that has gathered on the soul so that God's light may once again shine freely.

To prepare for Christ's coming is to invite peace back into our hearts. Sin and worry weigh us down, but confession and prayer restore us to grace. Each time we kneel before the Lord and ask for forgiveness, He fills the empty spaces of our hearts with His mercy. The peace that follows true repentance is unlike any other — it is the peace of being reconciled with God, of standing once again in the light of His love.

It is easy to think of peace as something passive — a soft, quiet feeling. But the peace of Christ is active and alive. It is the fruit of surrender. It comes when we stop resisting His will and begin to walk in harmony with His plan for us. When we align our hearts with His truth, even the storms of life cannot disturb the stillness within.

Consider how Mary prepared for Christ's coming. Her heart was open, pure, and ready. She welcomed the Word of God without hesitation, saying, *"Be it done unto me according to thy word."* (Luke 1:38). Her peace came not because she knew what lay ahead, but because she trusted completely in God's goodness. We, too, are called to prepare with that same openness — to trust that whatever God asks of us, His grace will provide.

Preparing our hearts also means extending peace to others. Advent is a time to mend what has been broken — to forgive those who have hurt us, to ask forgiveness where we have caused pain, and to seek reconciliation. Christ cannot fully enter a heart that clings to resentment or bitterness. To make room for the Prince of Peace, we must first become instruments of His peace.

The more we prepare our hearts, the more deeply we will experience the joy of Christmas. When we welcome Christ through prayer, repentance, and love, His peace transforms not just our emotions but our entire way of living. The restless heart finds rest, the anxious mind finds calm, and the weary soul finds renewal.

So let today be a day of spiritual preparation. Step away from the noise of the world, if only for a few moments, and ask the Lord to show you what in your heart needs to be made straight, healed, or renewed. Invite Him to sweep away the distractions that steal your peace and to plant within you a longing for His presence.

The King is near. He desires not a perfect heart, but a willing one — a heart open enough for His grace to enter.

Reflection:

True peace begins with preparation. When we turn back to God, we are not moving toward restriction, but toward freedom. The path of repentance is the road to peace because it removes what separates us from divine love.

Take time today to examine your heart. What worries, habits, or hurts are keeping you from the peace Christ desires to give you? Bring them before Him in prayer. The Lord never turns away a humble heart.

Advent is the perfect time to make a sincere confession, to renew your prayer life, and to simplify your spirit. As you prepare your heart, remember: you are not alone in this journey. The same God who called John to prepare the way is calling you now — gently, lovingly — to make room for His Son.

Prayer:

Lord Jesus,
You are the Prince of Peace, and You long to dwell within my heart. Yet I know that there are places within me still unprepared for Your coming. Cleanse me, Lord, from all that keeps me far from You. Wash me in Your mercy, and renew my spirit with Your grace.

Help me to turn away from sin and to walk in Your light. Teach me to forgive as You forgive, to love as You love, and to seek peace in every word and action. Let my heart become a manger where You may rest — humble, open, and filled with love.

As I journey through this week of Advent, may Your peace take root within me. Prepare me, O Lord, so that when You come, You will find my heart ready and my soul rejoicing.

Come, Lord Jesus, dwell in me and make me Your own.
Amen.

Thursday: Reconciliation and Forgiveness

Scripture Reading:

"If you are offering your gift at the altar and there remember that your brother has something against you, leave your gift there before the altar and go. First be reconciled to your brother, and then come and offer your gift."
— **Matthew 5:23–24**

The soft glow of the **Candle of Peace** reminds us that peace cannot fully dwell in a divided heart. The second week of Advent invites us not only to prepare for Christ's coming but to make peace with others — to seek reconciliation and forgiveness in every relationship. For how can we welcome the Prince of Peace if we refuse to live in His spirit of mercy?

Forgiveness lies at the very heart of the Gospel. It is both a gift we receive and a gift we are called to give. Jesus came to reconcile humanity to the Father, bridging the chasm that sin had created. Through His life, death, and resurrection, He restored peace between God and man. Now, as His followers, we are invited to continue that mission of reconciliation in our own lives — forgiving as we have been forgiven.

Advent is the perfect season to reflect on this. Just as the prophets urged the people to prepare their hearts, so Christ calls us to clear away resentment and bitterness that may have taken root within us. Holding onto anger, hurt, or pride closes the door to peace. Forgiveness, on the other hand, opens it wide — allowing God's grace to flow freely through our lives.

Forgiveness does not always come easily. Sometimes the wounds run deep, the pain feels fresh, and our hearts resist letting go. But forgiveness is not about denying the hurt or pretending nothing happened. It is about choosing love over revenge, healing over hatred, and grace over grudges. It is about freeing ourselves from the heavy weight of resentment and placing the matter into God's hands.

The truth is, when we refuse to forgive, we remain prisoners of the past. But when we forgive — even when the other person does not ask for it — we release ourselves into the freedom of God's peace. Forgiveness is not weakness; it is strength born from love. It takes courage to say, "I will no longer allow this pain to define me. I will let Christ's love define me instead."

In the same way, we also need to ask for forgiveness when we have wronged others. Pride often keeps us from admitting fault, but reconciliation begins with humility. Just as we long for mercy from God, we must be willing to extend and seek it from one another. Every act of reconciliation mirrors the love of the Father, who is always ready to welcome His children home.

Consider the Sacrament of Reconciliation — that sacred encounter where we confess our sins and receive absolution from the Lord. It is one of the greatest sources of peace we can experience. In confession, we lay down the burdens of guilt and walk away renewed. The peace that flows from that moment is not just emotional relief; it is the deep peace of being restored to friendship with God. If it has been a while since your last confession, let this Advent be the time you return. The Savior who waits in the confessional is the same Savior who was born in Bethlehem — gentle, merciful, and full of love.

When we allow God's mercy to wash over us, it becomes easier to share that mercy with others. The peace of forgiveness multiplies; the more we give, the more we receive.

To forgive is to imitate Christ. Hanging on the cross, in His deepest agony, He spoke words that changed the world: *"Father, forgive them, for they know not what they do."* (Luke 23:34). Those words were not just for His persecutors; they are for us — for every soul in need of mercy, for every heart longing for peace.

Reflection:

Forgiveness is the door through which peace enters. Without it, even the most beautiful prayers feel hollow. The Lord reminds us that before we bring our offerings to Him, we must first be reconciled to our brothers and sisters. Peace with God and peace with others are inseparable.

Take time today to examine your heart. Is there someone you need to forgive? Is there someone from whom you need to ask forgiveness? Bring that person to prayer. Ask the Lord to soften your heart and give you the grace to act with humility and love.

Advent is not only about waiting for the Lord's coming — it is about preparing a place where His love can dwell freely. And that place begins with a heart reconciled to God and to others.

Prayer:

Merciful Lord,
You are the source of all peace and forgiveness. You reconciled us to Yourself through the blood of Your Son and taught us to forgive one another as You have forgiven us.

Today, I bring before You every relationship that needs healing. Where there is anger, bring understanding. Where there is hurt, bring compassion. Where there is silence, bring courage to speak. Teach me to let go of resentment and to forgive with sincerity of heart.

If I have wronged others, grant me the humility to seek their pardon. Restore broken friendships, mend divided families, and fill our hearts with Your peace.

Lord Jesus, Prince of Peace, help me to live in harmony with all. Let my heart be a dwelling place for Your mercy, and may Your peace flow through me to those around me.

Come, Lord Jesus — reconcile what is broken, heal what is wounded, and make all things new.
Amen.

Friday: Prayer for Inner Calm

Scripture Reading:

"Do not be anxious about anything, but in everything by prayer and supplication with thanksgiving let your requests be made known to God. And the peace of God, which surpasses all understanding, will guard your hearts and your minds in Christ Jesus."
— **Philippians 4:6–7**

There are few things more precious in life than inner calm — that deep and quiet peace that remains even when everything around us is unsettled. This is the peace of Christ, the calm that comes not from escaping life's struggles, but from inviting God into them. As the **Candle of Peace** continues to shine this week, we are reminded that true calm is not found in control, but in surrender.

The Advent season can be both beautiful and overwhelming. The days grow shorter, the lists grow longer, and our hearts can easily become burdened by responsibilities and expectations. But in the midst of the noise, God calls us to stillness. He whispers softly, *"Be still, and know that I am God."* (Psalm 46:10). In that stillness, our souls are renewed, and peace finds a home within us again.

61

The peace that Christ offers is not a fleeting comfort or a momentary relief. It is a spiritual strength that anchors us in His love. St. Paul reminds us that this peace "surpasses all understanding" — meaning, it defies logic. It is the calm that fills us when we should be afraid, the strength that steadies us when we should crumble, the joy that rises even in sorrow. This peace is not something we create; it is something we receive when we open our hearts in prayer.

When anxiety begins to creep in, prayer becomes our lifeline. Prayer lifts our gaze from the problem to the presence of God. It reminds us that we are not alone, that every burden we carry can be laid at the feet of Christ. The act of prayer itself — whether whispered words, a silent sigh, or a tearful plea — opens the door to peace. God does not always change our circumstances, but He changes **us** within them.

Think of the storm on the Sea of Galilee. The disciples panicked as the waves crashed and the wind howled, but Jesus was asleep — completely calm. When they woke Him in fear, He simply said, *"Peace, be still,"* and the storm obeyed. (Mark 4:39). The same Lord who spoke peace to the waters speaks that same peace into our hearts today. When we trust Him, even our inner storms must grow quiet.

Inner calm begins with faith. It grows through prayer and is sustained by gratitude. St. Paul urges us not just to pray, but to pray **with thanksgiving**. Gratitude softens the heart and makes room for peace to dwell. When we thank God — even for small blessings — we shift our focus from what is missing to what has been given. Gratitude invites joy, and joy prepares the heart for peace.

To live in inner calm does not mean life will be free of trouble. It means that even in difficulty, we can rest in the presence of God who holds all things in His hands. The storms may still rage, but when our hearts are anchored in Christ, we will not be moved.

This Advent, let us learn to rest more and worry less. Let us practice sitting in silence before the Lord, breathing in His peace, and exhaling every fear. The world will always offer reasons to be anxious, but Christ offers us Himself — the perfect peace that quiets the mind and renews the soul.

When you light your candle today, imagine placing all your worries in the flame — letting them rise like incense before God. As the smoke fades into the air, trust that your prayers, too, have reached His heart.

Reflection:

Inner calm is not found in the absence of noise, but in the presence of God. It is possible to be surrounded by chaos and still carry peace within your soul. That kind of peace is a gift — one that grows each time you choose faith over fear, prayer over panic, and surrender over control.

Ask yourself: *What keeps me from resting in God's peace? Do I allow fear or busyness to drown out His still, small voice?*

The Lord's peace is available to you in every moment. You need only to stop, breathe, and invite Him in.

Prayer:

Lord Jesus,
You are my peace in every storm, my calm in every chaos.
When my heart is restless and my thoughts are heavy, teach
me to rest in You.

Quiet the noise within me, O Lord. Remove the worries
that weigh upon my spirit, and fill me with the serenity that
comes from Your presence alone. Help me to trust You
with all that troubles me, knowing that You are faithful and
good.

Teach me to bring my concerns to You in prayer and to
leave them there, confident that You are working for my
good. Replace my anxiety with gratitude, my fear with
faith, and my unrest with stillness.

Come, Prince of Peace, and dwell within me. Let Your
calm flow through my soul and radiate outward to all
whom I meet. May my life become a reflection of Your
peace in this weary world.

I rest in You, Lord — now and forever.
Amen.

Saturday: Peace on Earth, Peace Within

Scripture Reading:

"Glory to God in the highest, and on earth peace among men with whom He is pleased."
— **Luke 2:14**

The week of peace draws to a close with the angels' ancient song — the proclamation that still echoes through the ages: *"Glory to God in the highest, and on earth peace."* It is the song that rang out over Bethlehem's fields on that holy night, the song that every Advent invites us to sing again — not only with our lips, but with our lives.

The message of peace that the angels declared was not just poetic; it was prophetic. It announced the arrival of the Prince of Peace, the One who would reconcile heaven and earth, God and humanity. Through Christ, the world received a gift greater than any it could ever earn — the peace of divine presence, the peace of forgiveness, the peace that dwells deep within a redeemed heart.

Yet, this peace is not merely a distant ideal or a sentimental feeling. It is a call — a mission. The peace that Christ brings into our hearts must also flow through us into the world around us. Advent peace is meant to spread. Once we have experienced the calm of God's mercy within, we are sent forth to become instruments of that peace — in our homes, our families, our communities, and even in places where division seems impossible to mend.

Peace on earth begins with peace within.
When the human heart is ruled by pride, resentment, or fear, there can be no lasting peace in the world. Wars may cease for a time, but inner turmoil continues. Christ came to heal this very wound — to teach us that peace begins not with governments or systems, but with hearts that are surrendered to Him. The kingdom of peace starts in the soul.

The peace of Christ is not weak or passive; it is courageous and transformative. It moves us to forgive when it hurts, to serve when it's inconvenient, and to love even those who may never love us back. It's the peace that looks beyond self and seeks the good of others. Jesus said, *"Blessed are the peacemakers, for they shall be called children of God."* (Matthew 5:9). To be a follower of Christ is to be a bearer of peace.

When we choose kindness instead of harshness, understanding instead of judgment, humility instead of pride, we bring a piece of heaven to earth. Every small act of peace ripples outward, touching lives we may never even see. In a world filled with noise and conflict, even one soul at peace with God becomes a light — a steady flame that pushes back the shadows.

This is why the Advent wreath grows brighter each week. Each new candle represents the light of Christ spreading — from hope to peace, from one heart to another, until the world glows with the light of His love. Our peace within becomes the world's peace when we allow His Spirit to work through us.

But this kind of peace is not achieved through human strength. It is a grace — the fruit of intimacy with God. The more we dwell in His presence, the more our hearts begin to reflect His stillness. And the more we live in that stillness, the more others will encounter His peace through us.

Advent reminds us that Christ's peace is not a fragile truce; it is a strong and living force. It is the reconciliation that mends what sin has torn, the compassion that heals what hatred has broken, and the love that unites what fear has divided.

Let this final day of the week be a prayerful reflection on that great mystery: that the same Christ who was born into a quiet Bethlehem night now longs to be born anew in every human heart — bringing peace on earth, one soul at a time.

Reflection:

The angels' message was both a celebration and a challenge. They announced peace not as a mere wish, but as a divine reality made possible through Christ. The question for us is whether that peace has truly taken root in our hearts — and whether we are helping it take root in the world.

Peace begins when we surrender our need to control, to be right, to hold onto resentment. It deepens when we listen, when we love, when we choose compassion. It grows when we remember that every person — even the difficult ones — is a child of God.

Ask yourself: *Am I living as an instrument of Christ's peace? Do my words, actions, and choices bring calm or conflict? Do I seek peace only when it's convenient, or am I willing to sow it even in hard soil?*

Peace within is a gift; peace on earth is our mission. Both begin at the same altar — the heart that welcomes Christ.

Prayer:

Heavenly Father,
You sent Your Son into the world to bring peace — not as the world gives, but as only You can give. As this week of peace draws to a close, I thank You for the calm You have placed within my heart.

Help me to carry that peace into the world. Make me an instrument of reconciliation, a messenger of compassion, and a witness of Your love. Where there is conflict, let me sow understanding. Where there is hatred, let me bring forgiveness. Where there is despair, let me shine with hope.

Lord Jesus, Prince of Peace, rule within me so that Your peace may rule through me. Let my heart reflect the stillness of Bethlehem, and let my life echo the song of the angels — *"Glory to God in the highest, and on earth peace."*

Holy Spirit, breathe Your peace over my thoughts, my words, and my actions. Unite the hearts of all people in love, so that the earth may truly reflect the harmony of heaven.

Come, Lord Jesus — bring peace within me and through me.
Amen.

Sunday: The Joy of God's Nearness

Scripture Reading:

"Rejoice in the Lord always; again I say, rejoice! The Lord is near."
— **Philippians 4:4–5**

The third Sunday of Advent is called **Gaudete Sunday**, from the Latin word *"Gaudete,"* meaning "Rejoice!" It marks a joyful turning point in our Advent journey. The penitential purple of the previous weeks gives way to rose — a color of gladness and light — symbolizing that the waiting is almost over, and the coming of Christ is near.

As we light the **Candle of Joy**, we are reminded that joy is not the same as mere happiness. Happiness depends on circumstances — on things going well, on our plans unfolding smoothly. Joy, however, is deeper. It flows from a relationship with God that remains steady even when life is uncertain. Joy is the fruit of knowing that we are loved by God and that He is near to us — not far away, not indifferent, but truly present in every moment.

The Apostle Paul, writing from prison, declared: *"Rejoice in the Lord always."* His joy was not built on comfort or success but on faith. He knew that the presence of Christ changes everything — even suffering becomes bearable, even sorrow becomes sacred when it is lived with God.

That is the joy of Advent — the joy that comes from knowing that the Lord is close. We are not waiting for a distant or abstract Savior; we are awaiting Emmanuel — *God with us.* His nearness is our peace, our strength, and our joy.

In the Scriptures, we see this joy reflected in many hearts. Mary rejoiced in her Magnificat: *"My soul magnifies the Lord, and my spirit rejoices in God my Savior."* (Luke 1:46–47). The unborn John the Baptist leapt for joy in Elizabeth's womb when he sensed the presence of Christ. The shepherds rejoiced when the angels announced the Good News of His birth. Wherever Christ draws near, joy follows.

True joy, then, is not something we create; it is something we receive. It blooms in hearts that recognize the presence of God. When we slow down and make space for prayer, gratitude, and reflection, we begin to notice His nearness — in small moments, in gentle mercies, in the people around us. And in that awareness, joy takes root.

But joy also requires trust. Sometimes it's hard to rejoice when life feels heavy, when prayers seem unanswered, or when the world appears full of unrest. Yet Advent joy is not blind optimism — it is faith that shines precisely in the darkness. It proclaims, "God is near, even here, even now." It reminds us that no matter how bleak the world may seem, the Light is coming — and nothing can overcome it.

We are invited to carry this joy within us and to share it generously. The joy of God's nearness is not meant to be kept; it is meant to radiate. Like the rose-colored candle that glows with warmth amid the purple, our joy should bring light to others. A smile, a word of encouragement, a kind gesture — all these can become channels of divine joy.

As we celebrate Gaudete Sunday, let us rejoice not in what we have or what we lack, but in who God is and how deeply He loves us. Joy does not ignore life's difficulties — it transforms them. It lifts our gaze from the temporary to the eternal, from our struggles to His steadfast love.

Christ's nearness is not a promise for tomorrow; it is a reality today. He is near in His Word, near in the Eucharist, near in every act of love and mercy. To rejoice in the Lord is to recognize Him in all things — and to let that recognition fill us with unshakable peace.

So, light your candle of joy with gratitude in your heart. Let its warm glow remind you that God is near, that His promises are true, and that His coming is cause for rejoicing.

Reflection:

The joy of Advent is both a gift and a choice. It is a gift because it flows from God's presence; it is a choice because we must open our hearts to receive it. Joy is not found by chasing after comfort or perfection but by resting in God's love right where we are.

Ask yourself: *Do I believe that God is truly near to me? Do I allow His presence to fill me with joy, even when life feels uncertain?*

Joy grows in the heart that remembers God's faithfulness. It deepens when we serve others, when we give thanks, and when we live in gratitude. The more we recognize His presence, the more we will find ourselves rejoicing — even in the simplest of things.

Prayer:

Loving Father,
Today, my heart rejoices in Your presence. Thank You for drawing near to me — for sending Your Son, Jesus Christ, to dwell among us. You are my joy and my strength, the reason I can smile even in times of trial.

Lord, teach me to rejoice in You always. Help me to see Your hand in every circumstance, to trust that You are working for my good, and to rest in Your unchanging love. Let my heart be like Mary's — joyful, humble, and full of praise.

May my life reflect the joy of Your nearness. Make me a bearer of joy to others — through my words, my kindness, and my compassion. Let those who meet me feel the warmth of Your presence through me.

Come, Lord Jesus, and fill my soul with the joy that never fades — the joy of knowing that You are near and that I am Yours.
Amen.

Monday: Joy in God's Promises

Scripture Reading:

"Though the fig tree does not blossom, and no fruit is on the vines… yet I will rejoice in the Lord, I will exult in the God of my salvation."
— **Habakkuk 3:17–18**

The third week of Advent continues to radiate with warmth as the **Candle of Joy** burns brightly, calling us to rejoice — not because everything in life is perfect, but because **God's promises are sure**. True joy does not come from what we see, but from what we believe. It springs from the certainty that the Lord, who has spoken, will surely fulfill His word.

From the very beginning of Scripture, God has revealed Himself as a promise-keeping God. He made a covenant with Abraham, promising descendants as numerous as the stars. He assured Moses that His presence would go before Israel. Through the prophets, He declared the coming of the Messiah. Every promise — spoken across centuries — found its "Yes" in Jesus Christ. (2 Corinthians 1:20).

Advent reminds us that we are people who live in the light of promise. Just as the people of Israel waited in faith for the Messiah, we too wait in joyful expectation for the fulfillment of all that God has spoken. And as we wait, we remember — every promise of God carries the fragrance of hope and the sound of joy.

The prophet Habakkuk gives us one of the most beautiful examples of joyful trust. Though everything around him appeared barren and bleak, he chose to rejoice. He looked beyond his circumstances to the unchanging character of God. His joy was not rooted in abundance, but in assurance — in knowing that God's salvation was certain.

So it must be for us. Our joy must rest not on what we possess, but on who God is. He is faithful when we are unsteady. He is constant when the world shifts. His promises are not delayed by uncertainty; they unfold in perfect time. Even when we do not yet see the fruit of His word, we can rejoice, for He has never failed His people.

Think of the Virgin Mary, whose entire life was built upon God's promises. When the angel announced that she would bear the Son of God, her response was not fear, but faith: *"Behold, I am the handmaid of the Lord; let it be to me according to your word."* (Luke 1:38). Her joy came not from understanding every detail, but from trusting every word of the Lord.

And that same joy is offered to us. Joy in God's promises means choosing to believe that His word is true, even when our eyes cannot yet see its fulfillment. It means rejoicing in the midst of waiting — confident that the God who promised salvation is still at work in every season of our lives.

Perhaps today, you find yourself waiting — for direction, for healing, for peace, for a breakthrough. Take heart. Advent waiting is not empty; it is expectant. The Lord never forgets His word. Like seeds beneath the winter soil, His promises are already alive, waiting for their appointed time to bloom.

Joy is the song that faith sings in the waiting. It declares, "I know God will do what He has said." It chooses gratitude over worry, praise over despair, and worship over impatience.

When we anchor our joy in God's promises, we find that no trial can steal it. The joy of the Lord becomes our strength (Nehemiah 8:10) — not because everything is easy, but because we trust the One who holds the outcome.

As you meditate on this truth, remember that every promise fulfilled in the birth of Christ assures us that God's promises to us are equally secure. The same God who kept His word to Mary, Joseph, and the shepherds will also keep His word to you. His faithfulness is unchanging.

Reflection:

Advent joy is not shallow cheerfulness — it is the deep confidence that God is faithful to His word. It grows when we look back on His past goodness and look forward to His future glory.

Ask yourself: *Do I trust God's promises even when I cannot yet see them? Do I rejoice in His faithfulness, or do I allow worry to cloud my joy?*

Take time today to recall specific promises from Scripture — those that remind you of God's love, His mercy, and His provision. Write them down, pray them aloud, and let your heart rest in them. Every promise is a love letter written by a faithful God to His beloved people.

Prayer:

Faithful Father,
Your promises are true, Your word unchanging, and Your love everlasting. I thank You for every promise You have spoken — those fulfilled in the past, those unfolding in the present, and those yet to come.

Teach me to find joy not in what I see, but in what I believe. When my faith grows weak, remind me of Your steadfastness. When the waiting feels long, let Your promises sustain me. Like Mary, help me to say "yes" to Your word and to rejoice in the assurance of Your goodness.

Lord, fill my heart with joyful trust. Let my lips praise You even in uncertainty, and let my life reflect confidence in Your divine plan. May Your promises be the foundation of my peace and the song of my soul.

Come, Lord Jesus — fulfill in me every good word You have spoken. Let my joy overflow, for You are faithful and true.
Amen.

Tuesday: The Shepherds' Song of Gladness

Scripture Reading:

"And the angel said to them, 'Do not be afraid; for behold, I bring you good news of great joy that will be for all the people. For to you is born this day in the city of David a Savior, who is Christ the Lord.'"
— **Luke 2:10–11**

The third week of Advent continues to glow with the light of joy — the joy of God's nearness, the joy of His promises, and now, the joy that bursts forth in song among the humble and the lowly. Today, we join the shepherds in the fields of Bethlehem, who were the first to hear heaven's joyful announcement: *"For to you is born this day a Savior."*

The shepherds were ordinary men, poor and often overlooked by society. Yet God chose them to receive the greatest message the world had ever heard. This choice itself reveals something wondrous about God's heart — He delights in bringing His light to those who dwell in darkness and His joy to those who feel forgotten. Heaven's first proclamation of the Messiah's birth did not echo in royal courts or grand temples, but in the quiet stillness of a pasture under the night sky.

Imagine that sacred moment. The shepherds, keeping watch over their flocks, suddenly saw the darkness split apart by a radiant light. The angel's voice rang out, breaking centuries of silence with words of peace and joy. And then — as if heaven itself could no longer contain its rejoicing — a multitude of angels appeared, singing: *"Glory to God in the highest, and on earth peace to those on whom His favor rests!"* (Luke 2:14).

That song was not just for the shepherds; it was for all humanity. It declared that the promise had been fulfilled, that salvation had come, and that God's love had entered the world in the form of a tiny, sleeping Child. The shepherds' joy was pure and immediate — they did not hesitate. The Gospel says they went *"with haste"* to find the newborn King (Luke 2:16). Their faith was simple, their obedience complete, and their hearts overflowing with gladness.

When they found the Child lying in the manger, their joy deepened into worship. They gazed upon the Savior of the world — not clothed in splendor, but wrapped in humility. That sight filled them with awe and wonder. They returned to their flocks rejoicing, *"glorifying and praising God for all the things they had heard and seen."* (Luke 2:20).

The shepherds' story teaches us a profound truth: joy comes when we respond to God's invitation with faith and humility. Their joy was not dependent on wealth, comfort, or position; it flowed from encountering Christ Himself. When we draw near to Jesus in prayer, in Scripture, in the Eucharist, or in acts of love, we, too, experience that same deep joy.

This is the joy that cannot be silenced — the joy that overflows into praise and sharing. The shepherds could not keep the Good News to themselves; they told everyone what they had seen. Real joy is always generous. It spreads naturally, like light from one candle to another. When Christ fills our hearts, His joy becomes contagious.

Perhaps you have known moments like this — when the presence of God became so real that you could not help but rejoice. That is what Advent is meant to rekindle within us: not a fleeting excitement, but a steady joy born of divine encounter.

The world today still stands in need of that shepherd-like joy — the kind that proclaims, "Christ has come, and He is here among us!" Many hearts are weary, distracted, or afraid. But we, like the shepherds, are called to carry the message of the angels into the world. Every word of kindness, every act of charity, every moment of witness becomes a continuation of that heavenly song: *"Glory to God in the highest!"*

So as you reflect on the shepherds' gladness, ask yourself: *Do I approach Christ with the same eagerness and humility? Do I share the joy of His presence with others?* Let their example inspire you to rejoice deeply and to spread that joy wherever you go.

Reflection:

The joy of the shepherds was not only an emotion — it was an encounter. They met the living God and could not contain their praise. In the same way, we are invited to seek Christ this Advent with open hearts, to recognize Him in the quiet and the ordinary, and to let our joy become a song that glorifies Him.

Even now, the Lord appears in humble places — in moments of prayer, in the face of the poor, in the beauty of the Eucharist, in the stillness of faith. When we truly encounter Him there, our hearts, too, will sing.

Take a moment to sit in quiet wonder, imagining the fields of Bethlehem. Hear the angel's voice. Feel the radiance of divine joy surrounding you. And then whisper a prayer of thanksgiving that this same Savior has come — not only for the shepherds, but for you.

Prayer:

Heavenly Father,
You revealed the Good News of great joy to humble shepherds in the stillness of the night. Thank You for choosing the simple and the lowly to receive the first announcement of Your Son's birth.

Lord, open my heart to receive that same joy. Let me hear again the song of the angels and remember that Christ has come for me. Fill me with gratitude and wonder as I ponder the gift of Your love made flesh in Jesus.

Like the shepherds, may I seek You eagerly and share the joy of Your presence with others. Let my life proclaim, "Glory to God in the highest!" through every act of kindness, every word of faith, and every song of praise.

Come, Lord Jesus — awaken in me the same gladness that filled the hearts of the shepherds. May Your joy shine

through me and bring light to a weary world.
Amen.

Wednesday: Rejoicing in Hope

Scripture Reading:

"May the God of hope fill you with all joy and peace in believing, so that by the power of the Holy Spirit you may abound in hope."
— **Romans 15:13**

As the **Candle of Joy** continues to burn brightly this week, its light reminds us that true joy and hope are inseparable. Joy gives strength to hope, and hope gives endurance to joy. Together, they form the song of every believer's heart: *God is faithful, and His promises will never fail.*

Advent is a season of waiting, but not of empty waiting — it is waiting filled with **hopeful joy**. We look back with gratitude for Christ's first coming in Bethlehem, and we look forward with confident expectation to His coming again in glory. The joy of Advent is not limited to the past or confined to the future; it lives in the present, in the heart that trusts that God is always working, even when we cannot yet see the outcome.

To rejoice in hope is to live in the joyful assurance that God's plan is unfolding perfectly, even through life's uncertainties. Hope tells us that the story is not over — that no darkness lasts forever, and that the light of Christ will always prevail. When we truly believe this, our hearts cannot help but rejoice.

The Apostle Paul's words in Romans are not mere encouragement; they are a prayer and a promise. He calls God *"the God of hope"* — the source from which all hope and joy flow. He prays that we would be filled with *"all joy and peace in believing,"* meaning that faith itself becomes the doorway through which divine joy enters our lives. The more we believe, the more deeply we experience joy — not because circumstances are perfect, but because we know Who holds them.

In Scripture, hope and joy always go hand in hand. Abraham rejoiced in hope when he believed that God would give him a son, even in his old age. Hannah rejoiced in hope when she prayed for a child and trusted that God heard her cry. Mary rejoiced in hope when she said yes to God's plan, not knowing all that her obedience would bring. Their joy was rooted not in what they saw, but in what they trusted.

In the same way, our joy grows when we place our hope not in the world's promises but in God's. The world offers temporary happiness — pleasures that fade, achievements that pass, and possessions that rust. But the hope we have in Christ endures forever. It cannot be shaken by disappointment, grief, or delay. It is a living hope, born of His resurrection and sustained by His Spirit.

Sometimes, hope requires courage. There are seasons when life feels heavy — when prayers seem unanswered, and faith feels like walking in the dark. Yet even then, joy remains possible. Why? Because joy is not the absence of hardship; it is the presence of Christ. When we remember that He is near, our hearts begin to rest again. The Spirit whispers within us: *"Be patient. God is not finished yet."*

Hope allows us to rejoice even in the waiting, because we know the One we are waiting for is faithful. Advent joy is a defiant kind of joy — a light that shines despite the shadows, a song that rises above the silence. It says, *"I will rejoice, because God is good, and His promises are true."*

As you continue your Advent journey, let this be your prayer: to live as a person of hope, to let that hope give birth to joy, and to let your joy bear witness to a world that desperately needs light. The joy that springs from hope is contagious; it radiates peace, kindness, and love. When people see the quiet gladness in your eyes, they glimpse the light of Christ shining within you.

Reflection:

To rejoice in hope is to choose joy before the miracle comes. It is to sing before the dawn, trusting that the sun will rise. This kind of faith does not ignore pain or deny hardship; it simply places them in the hands of a faithful God and rests in His timing.

Ask yourself today: *Do I let hope guide my heart, or do I allow fear and impatience to steal my joy?* Hope is not wishful thinking; it is confident expectation rooted in God's faithfulness.

Let your prayer today be one of thanksgiving for the promises already fulfilled — and one of joyful hope for those yet to come.

Prayer:

God of Hope,
You are my joy and my strength. Thank You for the promises that never fail and the mercy that never ends. Fill my heart with Your peace as I wait for the fulfillment of all You have spoken.

When my spirit grows weary, renew me with Your hope. When my faith wavers, remind me of Your faithfulness. Help me to rejoice even in the waiting, knowing that Your plans are perfect and Your timing is good.

Let my joy in You be unshaken by circumstances and my hope be unwavering, rooted in Your eternal love. May the light of Your joy within me bring hope to others who struggle to believe.

Come, Lord Jesus — fill my life with joyful hope and make my heart sing with trust in You.
Amen.

Thursday: Gratitude in the Waiting

Scripture Reading:

"Give thanks in all circumstances; for this is the will of God in Christ Jesus for you."
— **1 Thessalonians 5:18**

As the **Candle of Joy** continues to shine this week, its flame calls us to a beautiful truth — that joy and gratitude are inseparable companions. Wherever gratitude is found, joy grows. Wherever joy flourishes, thanksgiving overflows. And nowhere is this more powerful than in the waiting.

Advent, at its heart, is a season of **waiting with gratitude**. We wait for the coming of Christ — not with restless impatience, but with thankful expectation. Gratitude turns waiting from frustration into worship, from anxiety into peace, from longing into joy. When we give thanks, even before we see the answer, we declare our faith that God is already at work.

It's easy to be thankful when life feels full — when prayers are answered, blessings are visible, and days are bright. But the truest form of gratitude is born in the quiet places of trust — when we thank God not for what we hold in our hands, but for who He is in our hearts. The Apostle Paul reminds us, *"Give thanks in all circumstances."* That means in joy and in sorrow, in abundance and in lack, in certainty and in mystery.

Gratitude does not mean ignoring hardship or pretending everything is easy. It means recognizing that even in the midst of trials, God remains good, faithful, and near. It is the posture of a heart that sees beyond the moment to the promise.

Think of Mary during her journey to Bethlehem. She was weary, heavily pregnant, and far from home, yet her heart still sang with gratitude: *"My soul magnifies the Lord, and my spirit rejoices in God my Savior."* (Luke 1:46–47). Her gratitude was not dependent on her comfort — it flowed from her trust. She knew that even in uncertainty, God's plan was unfolding perfectly.

Gratitude transforms waiting because it shifts our focus from what we lack to what we have already been given. It reminds us that every breath, every sunrise, every act of love is a gift. Even the waiting itself becomes a blessing, for it draws us closer to God's heart. In thanksgiving, our hearts become softer, our eyes clearer, and our faith stronger.

The world often teaches us to wait with impatience — to measure time by what we have not yet received. But Advent teaches us to wait with wonder — to measure time by what God is preparing in love. Gratitude is what bridges that waiting; it keeps our hearts open and our spirits joyful even when the journey feels long.

When we practice gratitude, joy deepens. Every small blessing becomes a spark of light. The warmth of friendship, the kindness of a stranger, the simple grace of a quiet moment — these are reminders that God's goodness is woven into the fabric of every day.

Even when our prayers seem unanswered, gratitude helps us trust that God is still writing our story — one filled with mercy, purpose, and grace. The waiting does not diminish His love; it prepares us to receive it more fully.

Reflection:

Gratitude in the waiting is one of the purest forms of worship. It says, "Lord, even before I see the miracle, I thank You for it." It turns waiting into a sacred space where faith grows and joy blooms.

Take a few moments today to reflect on the blessings God has already given you — both big and small. Write them down if you can. You may be surprised to see how many reasons you have to be thankful. Gratitude is not just a feeling; it is a practice. The more we give thanks, the more our hearts are shaped by joy.

Ask yourself: *Do I fill my waiting with thanksgiving, or do I fill it with worry? Do I see God's goodness even when His timing is slow?*

Choose today to say "thank You" — not because everything is perfect, but because God is.

Prayer:

Gracious and Loving Father,
Thank You for the countless blessings You pour into my
life — for the gifts I can see and for those still hidden in
Your plan. Even in the waiting, I know You are good. Even
in uncertainty, I know You are near.

Teach me to be thankful in all circumstances. When my
heart is anxious, remind me of Your faithfulness. When I
grow impatient, fill me with Your peace. Let my gratitude
be a song of praise that rises to You each day.

Like Mary, may I rejoice in Your goodness even when I
cannot yet see the full picture. Transform my waiting into
worship, my longing into trust, and my silence into joyful
expectation.

Come, Lord Jesus — fill my heart with gratitude and joy as
I await Your coming.
Amen.

Friday: Spreading Joy and Kindness

"Let your light so shine before men, that they may see your good works and glorify your Father who is in heaven."
— **Matthew 5:16**

The soft, rose-colored flame of the **Candle of Joy** continues to glow, illuminating our path as Advent draws us closer to the celebration of Christ's birth. By now, our hearts have been filled with the joy of God's nearness, the joy of His promises, and the joy of gratitude in the waiting. Today, we are reminded that this joy is not meant to remain hidden within us — it is meant to shine outward. Joy, when rooted in God's love, naturally overflows into **kindness**.

Joy and kindness are inseparable companions. Where true joy lives, kindness blooms. When the heart is filled with Christ, it cannot help but give. The same God who fills us with His joy calls us to spread it to others — to become messengers of His goodness in a world that often feels weary and cold.

During Advent, our call is to reflect the light of Christ in both word and deed. Just as the angels shared the "good news of great joy," we too are called to bring that joy into the lives of those around us. Every smile offered, every kind word spoken, every act of compassion extended becomes a spark of divine light in someone else's darkness.

Sometimes we underestimate how powerful small acts of kindness can be. A listening ear, a warm meal, a helping hand — these gestures might seem simple, but in God's eyes, they are radiant. They carry His love to others and remind them that He has not forgotten them. The world is full of heavy hearts longing for even a glimmer of hope. When we act with kindness, we become bearers of that hope.

Advent kindness is not just about giving gifts or performing good deeds; it's about giving ourselves. It's about showing patience when we'd rather hurry, offering forgiveness when it's hard, and extending love without expecting anything in return. These are the gifts that mirror the heart of Christ — gifts that bring lasting joy.

Look to Jesus as our perfect example. His life was one continuous outpouring of love and kindness. He touched the sick, comforted the broken, welcomed the outcast, and blessed those who least expected it. Everywhere He went, joy followed, because kindness and love radiated from His every action. As His disciples, we are called to do the same.

When we spread joy and kindness, we participate in the mystery of Christmas itself — the mystery of God's love taking on flesh and dwelling among us. Every time we choose compassion over indifference, gentleness over irritation, generosity over selfishness, we make Christ visible in the world.

It is especially in this holy season that our kindness can become a reflection of God's love to others. The lonely neighbor, the struggling parent, the discouraged friend — all need reminders that joy still exists, that light still shines, and that Christ still comes to us in love. Our kindness can be that reminder.

The candle of joy burns brighter when it is shared. It is not diminished by giving; it multiplies. The more we spread joy, the more our own hearts are filled. Joy grows through kindness because it is the language of heaven — the echo of divine love reaching from one heart to another.

Reflection:

Spreading joy and kindness is not about doing grand or heroic things — it's about doing small things with great love. It's about making space in our hearts for others, especially those who may be forgotten or overlooked.

Ask yourself today: *Whom can I bless with kindness? How can I make someone's day brighter? Where can I bring joy where there is heaviness?*

Every act of love you offer becomes a prayer — a living testimony of the joy that Christ has placed within you. The light of Advent joy is not meant to be kept under a basket; it's meant to shine for all to see.

Let your joy be contagious. Let your kindness be genuine. And let your life quietly say, "Christ is near."

Prayer:

Lord Jesus,
You are the Light of the world and the source of all joy.
Thank You for filling my heart with Your presence and for
teaching me that true joy grows when it is shared.

Help me to spread Your love through simple acts of
kindness. Open my eyes to see those who are lonely,
burdened, or forgotten. Give me the courage to reach out
with compassion, to speak words of encouragement, and to
serve with a willing heart.

Let my joy reflect Yours — humble, generous, and pure.
May every act of kindness I offer this day bring light to
others and glory to Your name.

Lord, make me a bearer of Advent joy wherever I go.
Come, Prince of Peace, fill me with Your love and help me
to share it freely.
Amen.

Saturday: The Heart of Joyful Service

Scripture Reading:

"Whoever wishes to be great among you must be your servant, and whoever wishes to be first among you must be your slave; just as the Son of Man came not to be served but to serve, and to give His life as a ransom for many."
— **Matthew 20:26–28**

As the **Candle of Joy** flickers brightly at the close of this third week of Advent, we are reminded that true joy is never self-centered — it is **others-centered**. Joy finds its deepest fulfillment not in what we receive, but in what we give. The heart that truly rejoices in Christ naturally expresses that joy through loving service to others.

In a world that often measures greatness by power, success, or recognition, Jesus redefines it entirely. He shows us that true greatness is found in humility, and that lasting joy flows from service. The Lord Himself — the King of Heaven — came not to be served but to serve. He washed the feet of His disciples, fed the hungry, healed the sick, and carried the burdens of the broken. Every act of service He performed was a reflection of divine love in motion.

When we serve others, we share in the joy of Christ. Service done with love is not a burden but a blessing. It fills our hearts with peace and purpose because it aligns us with the very heart of God. Serving transforms ordinary moments into sacred ones — a smile offered to a stranger, a meal shared with someone in need, a word of comfort to the weary. In each of these, Christ's love is made visible.

Advent is a perfect time to renew our call to serve joyfully. This season reminds us that God's greatest gift to humanity came through service — the service of a humble Savior who entered the world not in glory, but in a manger. He did not demand honor; He gave Himself completely. And in that gift, the world found joy everlasting.

To serve joyfully, we must first serve from the heart. True service flows not from obligation but from love. It is not about seeking praise, but about seeking to bless. The more we give, the freer we become — because love, when poured out, multiplies rather than diminishes.

Consider Mary, who after receiving the news that she would bear the Savior, *"arose and went with haste"* to serve Elizabeth (Luke 1:39). Her first act after receiving God's promise was an act of service. Her heart was full of joy, and that joy immediately expressed itself in love for another. Joy and service are intertwined — joy fuels service, and service deepens joy.

Every Christian is called to live this way — to see every opportunity to serve as an invitation to encounter Christ. When we serve others, we are not simply performing tasks; we are ministering to Christ Himself. *"Whatever you did for one of the least of these my brothers, you did it for Me."* (Matthew 25:40).

Sometimes service requires sacrifice. It may mean giving up time, comfort, or resources. But the reward is far greater — the quiet joy of knowing we have reflected the love of God in a world that desperately needs it. And that kind of joy endures long after the act itself.

As this week of joy draws to a close, let us remember that joyful service is not limited to the Advent season. It is a way of life — a daily response to the love we have received. Christ's joy is not meant to stay within the walls of our hearts; it is meant to move through our hands and feet, touching lives with gentleness and grace.

Reflection:

The heart of joyful service is gratitude. We serve not because we must, but because we have already been so abundantly loved by God. Every act of service becomes a way of saying, "Thank You, Lord, for loving me first."

Ask yourself today: *How can I serve with joy? Whom can I bless with my time, attention, or care?* The Lord may be calling you to a simple act — helping a neighbor, visiting the lonely, or showing patience to someone difficult to love. These small acts of service are where true discipleship begins.

When we serve with joy, our lives become a living reflection of the Gospel — a silent yet powerful proclamation that Christ is near.

Prayer:

Lord Jesus,
You are the Servant King, who came not to be served but to serve. Teach me to follow Your example with humility and love. Let my joy overflow in acts of kindness, compassion, and care for others.

Free my heart from selfishness and pride, and fill it instead with gratitude for all You have done for me. Help me to see every opportunity to serve as a gift — a chance to share Your light with someone in need.

When serving feels difficult or unnoticed, remind me that You see every act of love. Strengthen me with Your Spirit so that my service may be done with a joyful heart and a willing spirit.

Come, Lord Jesus — dwell in me and make my hands Your hands, my words Your words, my heart Your heart. May my life be a living act of joyful service to You and to others.
Amen.

Sunday: The Love that Redeems

Scripture Reading:

"For God so loved the world that He gave His only begotten Son, that whoever believes in Him should not perish but have everlasting life."
— **John 3:16**

As the final candle of the Advent wreath is lit — the **Candle of Love** — its warm, gentle glow fills the circle, completing the light that began weeks ago with hope, peace, and joy. Each flame leads us here, to the heart of Advent's mystery: **love — divine, redeeming, unconditional love**.

This final Sunday of Advent invites us to gaze upon the love that redeems — the love that moved heaven to earth, the love that took on flesh and dwelt among us. It is a love so vast that it cannot be measured, a love so pure that it sought us when we were lost, and a love so powerful that it conquered sin and death.

From the beginning of time, God's love has been the thread running through the story of salvation. He created us out of love, called us back when we strayed, and promised redemption through His Son. Every prophecy, every covenant, every act of mercy throughout Scripture pointed to this moment — the coming of Love Himself.

The love that redeems is not a distant or abstract affection; it is love in action. It is the love that kneels to wash feet, that weeps at the tomb, that forgives even from the cross. It is the love that restores dignity to the broken and calls sinners "beloved." It is the love that bears all things, believes all things, hopes all things, endures all things. (1 Corinthians 13:7).

In sending His Son into the world, God did not simply offer comfort — He offered **salvation**. His love does not merely console us; it transforms us. Redemption means that what was once bound by sin is now set free, that what was once darkened by despair now shines with divine light. The manger and the cross are both symbols of this redeeming love — love that stooped low enough to enter our world and strong enough to lift us back to heaven.

As we stand on the threshold of Christmas, this is the truth that stirs our hearts: **we are loved beyond measure.** God's love is not dependent on our worthiness; it flows freely from His mercy. Advent's final invitation is not only to believe in that love but to let it change us — to live as people redeemed, to see ourselves and others through the eyes of that love.

When we meditate on this redeeming love, our hearts cannot remain indifferent. Love that great demands a response. And our response, like Mary's, must be one of surrender and trust: *"Be it done unto me according to Thy word."* (Luke 1:38). Her "yes" opened the door for the Redeemer to enter the world. Our "yes" allows His redeeming love to continue working in and through us today.

The love that redeems does not remain hidden; it radiates outward. It compels us to forgive as we have been forgiven, to serve as we have been served, and to love even those who are hardest to love. When we allow Christ's love to fill us, it overflows into every relationship, every word, every action.

And so, as we light the Candle of Love, let it remind us of what all the waiting, hoping, and rejoicing have led to — the revelation of divine love made visible in the face of a newborn Child. This is not just the love that comforts; it is the love that **redeems**, the love that saves.

Reflection:

God's redeeming love is the foundation of our faith. It is the love that finds us in our weakness and lifts us into grace. Advent is not only about preparing for Christ's birth but about rediscovering the depth of that love and letting it renew our hearts.

Ask yourself today: *Do I truly believe that God's love is greater than my failures? Do I allow His love to redeem the broken parts of my heart?*

When we open ourselves to this love, it changes how we see everything — ourselves, others, and even the hardships of life. The love that redeems gives us strength to forgive, courage to trust, and peace to rest in God's will.

As this final week begins, take time each day to rest in the truth of His love. Whisper a prayer of gratitude for the gift of redemption. Let His love wash over you, heal you, and send you forth as a bearer of that same love to others.

Prayer:

Redeeming Lord,
Your love is beyond measure, beyond reason, beyond words. You came to save not because we deserved it, but because You could not stop loving us. Thank You for sending Your Son — Love made flesh — to redeem us and draw us back to Your heart.

Teach me to live in the freedom of that love. Heal the places in me that are wounded, and fill my heart with Your mercy. Help me to see myself and others through Your eyes — beloved, forgiven, redeemed.

May Your love flow through me to those who need it most. Let me be patient, gentle, and kind, reflecting the heart of Christ in all that I do.

Come, Lord Jesus, Love Incarnate. Dwell within me and let Your redeeming love shine through my life.
Amen.

Monday: God's Love Made Visible

Scripture Reading:

"The Word became flesh and dwelt among us, and we have seen His glory, the glory of the one and only Son, who came from the Father, full of grace and truth."
— **John 1:14**

The **Candle of Love** burns with a soft, radiant light — a reminder that all of God's promises, all of history's longing, and all of creation's hope have found their fulfillment in one breathtaking truth: **God's love became visible.**

This is the heart of the Gospel and the wonder of Christmas — that the infinite God, Creator of heaven and earth, humbled Himself to take on human flesh. The Word that spoke galaxies into existence became a Child, wrapped in swaddling clothes, laid in a manger. The invisible became visible. The Almighty became approachable. The Divine became human.

In the birth of Jesus, God's love took shape, face, and form. He didn't send an angel, a prophet, or a symbol — He came Himself. Love didn't stay distant; it entered into our story.

Every heartbeat of the infant Christ was the rhythm of divine love pulsing through human life. In Him, God's heart was made visible to the world.

The Incarnation is not just a moment in history; it is a revelation of who God is — **Love made visible, love made personal, love made near.** He did not come to impress us with power or overwhelm us with majesty; He came to embrace us with tenderness, to dwell among us, and to show us the face of mercy.

When we look at Jesus — at His compassion for the sick, His kindness toward the sinner, His patience with the lost — we see the very character of God revealed. Every word He spoke, every hand He reached out, every tear He shed was the visible expression of an invisible love.

This is why Christmas is not merely a celebration of a birth; it is a celebration of **the love that came down from heaven to walk beside us.** In Christ, God's love has a voice that speaks our language, hands that can touch our wounds, and a heart that understands our pain. He came to share our joys and sorrows, to sanctify every human experience with His divine presence.

When we say that "God's love became visible," we are also reminded that love is meant to be seen — to take form through our actions, to be expressed in mercy, compassion, and truth. Christ's coming calls us to live as reflections of that same visible love.

Our faith is not meant to be hidden; it is meant to shine. Just as God's love took on flesh in Jesus, we are invited to make His love visible in the world today — through our kindness, our forgiveness, our generosity, and our courage to care. When we feed the hungry, comfort the lonely, forgive the offender, or pray for the suffering, we continue the work of the Incarnation.

Each act of love becomes a mirror of God's heart — a reminder that His light still shines in the world. The more we allow His love to dwell in us, the more others will see Him through us. Advent prepares us for this mission: to carry the love that became visible in Bethlehem into every corner of the earth.

The world is longing for visible love. It is weary of words without compassion and faith without action. People hunger for signs of mercy, for hearts that reflect the tenderness of Christ. As disciples, we are called to be those signs — living witnesses of Emmanuel, *God with us.*

So as we enter this final stretch of Advent, let us gaze upon the manger and remember: that tiny Child is Love Himself — pure, humble, eternal. And His light still shines in every act of love we offer in His name.

Reflection:

When love becomes visible, it transforms everything it touches. It softens hearts, heals wounds, and turns darkness into light.

Ask yourself: *How am I making God's love visible in my life today? Do others see His kindness and mercy through my words and actions?*

God's love is not meant to be admired from a distance; it is meant to be lived. Let your daily life — your home, your work, your friendships — become the place where His love takes flesh again.

Remember: Every moment of compassion is a reflection of the Incarnation. Every act of mercy is Christmas renewed.

Prayer:

Loving Father,
You revealed Your heart to the world through Jesus, Your Son — Love made visible, Love made flesh. Thank You for coming so close, for stepping into our humanity so that we might share in Your divinity.

Teach me to live as a reflection of that love. Let my words speak kindness, my hands offer help, and my heart show mercy. May others see in me a glimpse of the love that first shone in Bethlehem.

Lord, help me to remember that You are not distant but near — living and dwelling in me. Strengthen me to bring Your love into every part of my life and to those who need it most.

Come, Lord Jesus — dwell visibly in me, so that through my life, Your love may shine into the world.
Amen.

Tuesday: Mary's Fiat – The Handmaid of the Lord

Scripture Reading:

"And Mary said, 'Behold, I am the handmaid of the Lord; let it be to me according to your word.' And the angel departed from her."
— **Luke 1:38**

As the **Candle of Love** continues to burn brightly in this final week of Advent, its light draws us into the mystery of one of the most profound moments in salvation history — Mary's *fiat*, her "yes" to God. In a simple, humble room in Nazareth, the eternal plan of redemption hinged upon the response of a young woman's heart. And through her surrender, love entered the world in flesh and blood.

Mary's "yes" was not merely a word; it was an offering. It was the complete surrender of her will to the will of God. In that moment of holy obedience, she became the first disciple of Christ — the first to receive Him, the first to carry His presence within her, and the first to proclaim His coming through the quiet witness of faith.

The angel Gabriel's message was astonishing. He told her she would conceive the Son of God through the Holy Spirit

— an unimaginable promise, one that defied human understanding. Yet Mary did not question God's power; she simply opened her heart and said, *"Let it be done to me according to Your word."* That response changed everything. Her surrender turned divine promise into human reality.

In Mary, we see the perfect model of love — a love that listens, trusts, and obeys. Her *fiat* teaches us that true love is not passive emotion but active faith. It is saying "yes" to God even when we don't understand His ways, trusting that His plan is always good. Love's truest expression is found in surrender.

Mary's surrender was not without cost. Her "yes" meant stepping into uncertainty — facing misunderstanding, possible rejection, and great suffering. Yet she chose love over fear. Her courage came not from knowing the future, but from knowing the One who held it. That is the heart of faith — and the secret of her peace.

When Mary called herself the "handmaid of the Lord," she accepted her role as a servant in God's great plan of salvation. Her humility was not weakness, but strength rooted in love. She trusted that even in her lowliness, God could work wonders. Indeed, her own words in the Magnificat proclaim it: *"He who is mighty has done great things for me, and holy is His name."* (Luke 1:49).

In Mary, we see that love and obedience are never in conflict — they are two sides of the same coin. To love God truly is to trust Him completely. Her *fiat* invites us to ask ourselves: *Am I willing to let God's will unfold in my life, even when it challenges my plans or expectations? Do I respond to His call with faith and love, or with hesitation and fear?*

Advent is a time to renew our own *yes* to God. Each of us is called, in our own way, to carry Christ into the world — to bear His love, His truth, and His light through our lives. Like Mary, we may not always understand what God asks of us, but we can trust that His grace will sustain us.

Every time we say "yes" to kindness, forgiveness, or compassion, we echo Mary's *fiat*. Every act of surrender, every prayer of trust, every moment we choose faith over fear becomes a small reflection of her love. Through our obedience, Christ continues to be made visible in the world.

The love that entered the world through Mary's *yes* continues to flow through every heart that welcomes Him. Her life is proof that when we yield to God's will, His love can accomplish the impossible.

Reflection:

Mary's *fiat* reminds us that love is not only a feeling but a decision — a choice to align our hearts with God's will, no matter the cost. It is saying, *"Lord, not my way, but Yours."*

Ask yourself: *How am I responding to God's invitations in my life? Am I open to His plan, or do I hold back in fear or pride?*

Let Mary's example inspire you to surrender with trust. God does not look for perfection — only for a willing heart. When we give Him our *yes*, He fills our lives with grace beyond measure.

Prayer:

Heavenly Father,
You chose Mary, humble and pure, to be the mother of
Your Son. In her *fiat*, You revealed the power of perfect
love — a love that listens, believes, and obeys.

Teach me to say "yes" to You as Mary did. Help me to trust
Your plan even when I do not see the path ahead. Give me
the courage to surrender my fears and desires into Your
hands, knowing that Your will is always for my good.

Lord, let Your love be conceived in my heart as it was in
Mary's. Make me a vessel of Your presence in the world —
bringing light where there is darkness, faith where there is
doubt, and hope where there is despair.

Come, Lord Jesus, dwell within me as You once dwelt
within Your Blessed Mother.
Amen.

Wednesday: Joseph's Silent Obedience

Scripture Reading:

"When Joseph woke from sleep, he did as the angel of the Lord commanded him; he took his wife, but knew her not until she had borne a son. And he called His name Jesus."
— **Matthew 1:24–25**

The **Candle of Love** continues to glow this week, and today its gentle flame invites us to reflect on the quiet, steadfast love of **Saint Joseph** — the man chosen by God to guard the Redeemer and care for the Blessed Virgin Mary. His story, though told in few words, speaks volumes. Joseph's love is not loud or showy; it is humble, faithful, and deeply obedient. It is love expressed not through words, but through action.

In Joseph, we see the embodiment of **silent obedience** — a love that listens more than it speaks, that acts more than it demands, and that trusts more than it understands. Though Scripture records not a single spoken word from him, his life echoes with the language of faith. Each decision he made was guided by his love for God and his willingness to do God's will, even when it defied human reason.

When Joseph first learned that Mary was with child, his heart must have been troubled. As a just man, he sought to do what was right, but his understanding of God's plan was incomplete. Yet even in confusion, Joseph chose compassion over condemnation. His first thought was to protect Mary, not to shame her — an act of mercy born of deep love.

Then, as he slept, an angel appeared to him in a dream and revealed the truth: *"Do not be afraid to take Mary as your wife, for that which is conceived in her is of the Holy Spirit."* (Matthew 1:20). Upon waking, Joseph did not argue or delay. He simply obeyed. In quiet faith, he accepted his role in God's divine plan — to be the earthly father of the Messiah and the protector of the Holy Family.

His obedience was not passive resignation but active trust. It required great courage and self-sacrifice. Joseph's "yes" to God meant embracing uncertainty, bearing misunderstanding, and walking a path few would comprehend. Yet through that obedience, God's love was safeguarded on earth. The infant Christ would grow up in a home marked by gentleness, faith, and strength — because Joseph's love was steady and true.

Joseph's silence is not emptiness; it is full of contemplation. In that silence, he listened for the voice of God. In that stillness, he discerned what love required. In that obedience, he became a model for every believer who seeks to love God with faith that acts even when words fail.

How needed this example is in our world today — a world filled with noise, opinions, and haste. Joseph teaches us that love does not always need to speak; sometimes, it simply needs to be faithful. The truest form of love often happens in hidden places — in quiet sacrifices, in daily responsibilities, in acts of service that no one sees but God.

The carpenter of Nazareth teaches us that holiness is found not only in great deeds but in ordinary faithfulness. By working with his hands, by protecting his family, by trusting in God's timing, Joseph lived out the Gospel long before it was preached. His life was a silent hymn of love — steady, enduring, and pure.

And just as Mary's "yes" allowed love to take flesh, Joseph's obedience ensured that love was protected and nurtured. His heart, though silent, beat in harmony with God's will. That is the mark of a true disciple — to listen, to trust, and to obey out of love.

Reflection:

Joseph's silent obedience challenges us to consider: *Do I listen for God's voice amid the noise of my daily life? Do I trust His direction, even when I don't understand it?*

Love and obedience are intertwined. True love seeks not its own way but God's. In the stillness of prayer, in the simplicity of our duties, we too can echo Joseph's faith — saying "yes" to God quietly, faithfully, and completely.

Remember: love does not need to make a sound to be strong. Sometimes, it is in silence that love speaks most clearly.

Prayer:

Heavenly Father,
You chose Saint Joseph to be the protector of Your Son and the guardian of Mary. Thank You for his example of humble strength, silent obedience, and steadfast love.

Teach me, Lord, to listen for Your voice in the quiet moments of life. When I do not understand Your will, help me to trust as Joseph did. When obedience feels difficult, give me the grace to act with courage and love.

Let my life, like Joseph's, be a quiet witness to Your faithfulness. May my love be patient, my heart steadfast, and my actions guided by Your Spirit.

Saint Joseph, protector of the Holy Family, pray for me — that I may love God faithfully, serve Him humbly, and obey Him completely.
Amen.

Thursday: The Gift of Charity and Compassion

Scripture Reading:

"Above all, clothe yourselves with love, which binds everything together in perfect harmony."
— **Colossians 3:14**

The **Candle of Love** continues to shine softly, reminding us that love is not only an emotion we feel but a gift we give. As Advent draws near its fulfillment, today's reflection calls us to live out that love in its most tangible form — through **charity and compassion**. These are the visible signs of a heart transformed by divine love, the fruit of a soul that has truly encountered Christ.

Charity, in its truest sense, is not simply generosity — it is love in action. It is the outward expression of an inward grace. The word *charity* comes from the Latin *caritas*, meaning "love" — the kind of selfless, sacrificial love that reflects God's own heart. When we act with charity and compassion, we are not just doing good deeds; we are participating in the very mission of Christ, who came to bring healing, comfort, and hope to the world.

Compassion goes even deeper. The word means "to suffer with." It is the ability to enter into another's pain, to feel what they feel, and to respond with tenderness. Jesus showed compassion wherever He went — feeding the hungry, healing the sick, comforting the grieving, forgiving the sinner. His miracles were not merely demonstrations of power; they were revelations of love. Every gesture, every word, every act of mercy was born of divine compassion.

As disciples of Christ, we are called to that same compassionate love. Advent reminds us that love is not confined to sentiment or ceremony. It is lived daily — in the way we treat others, in the patience we show, in the generosity we extend, and in the kindness we choose.

To live with charity and compassion is to imitate the heart of God. It means noticing those who are overlooked, helping those who are struggling, and giving from a place of love rather than duty. It means asking not "What do I have to give?" but "Whom can I love today?"

When we open our hearts in this way, we discover that every act of compassion — no matter how small — becomes a doorway for God's grace. A smile to the lonely, a listening ear to the weary, a meal for the hungry, a prayer for the forgotten — each is a seed of love that can blossom into something eternal.

Charity is also an act of faith. It proclaims to the world that God's love is still alive — alive in us. Every time we give, forgive, or extend kindness, we bear witness to Emmanuel — *God with us.* The love we share becomes a continuation of the love that began in Bethlehem.

During Advent, as we prepare our hearts for Christ's birth, we must also prepare to recognize Him in the faces of others — especially those in need. Christ comes to us disguised in many forms: the poor, the sick, the lonely, the sorrowful. When we show compassion to them, we are not merely helping people; we are serving the Lord Himself. *"Whatever you did for one of the least of these my brothers, you did it for Me."* (Matthew 25:40).

This is the essence of love — to see Christ in everyone and to love without counting the cost. Charity without compassion can become cold obligation, but compassion without charity can remain mere feeling. The two must work together, forming the perfect bond of love that unites us to God and to one another.

So as you light your candle of love today, remember: every act of charity and compassion kindles the light of Christ in a world that often feels cold and dark. Love multiplies when it is given away. Let your love be active, your compassion sincere, and your kindness overflowing.

Reflection:

Charity and compassion are not optional virtues for Christians — they are the heartbeat of the Gospel. To love as Christ loves is to give of ourselves freely, even when it costs us something. It is to see others not as problems to solve, but as souls to cherish.

Ask yourself: *Who around me needs to experience the warmth of God's love today? How can I show compassion to someone who is hurting or alone?*

True love is not measured by the size of the gift but by the depth of the heart that gives it. Even the smallest act of kindness can become a channel of divine grace.

Prayer:

Loving Father,
You have shown me perfect love through Your Son, Jesus Christ, who gave Himself completely for me. As I reflect on Your great love, teach me to love others with that same generosity and compassion.

Fill my heart with Your tenderness, so that I may see others through Your eyes. Give me hands that serve, a heart that forgives, and a spirit that gives freely without seeking reward.

Lord, help me to live this day in love — to be patient with those who frustrate me, gentle with those who struggle, and merciful with those in need. Let my actions speak louder than my words, and let my compassion draw others closer to You.

Come, Lord Jesus — fill me with Your love, that I may be a living sign of Your charity and compassion in the world. **Amen.**

Friday: The Word Made Flesh

Scripture Reading:

"And the Word became flesh and dwelt among us, and we have seen His glory, the glory as of the only begotten of the Father, full of grace and truth."
— **John 1:14**

As the **Candle of Love** burns brightly on this final Friday of Advent, its warm, steady flame points us toward the greatest mystery ever revealed — the **Incarnation**, when the eternal Word of God became flesh and lived among us. This is the very heart of our faith, the moment when divine love entered time and took on the form of humanity.

For generations, humanity waited in darkness, yearning for redemption, longing for the voice of God to break through the silence. Then, in a quiet town and in a humble stable, the Word that spoke creation into existence took His first human breath. The One who fashioned the stars became a child. The infinite became small. The all-powerful became vulnerable. And through this miracle, **love became visible, tangible, and everlasting.**

John's Gospel opens not with a manger scene or shepherds in the fields but with this divine declaration — *"In the beginning was the Word, and the Word was with God, and the Word was God."* (John 1:1). The same Word that said "Let there be light" at creation spoke once again in Bethlehem — not through thunder or fire, but through the cry of a newborn baby. The Word that once created life had now come to **redeem** it.

The mystery of the Incarnation reveals how far God's love will go to reach us. He did not send a messenger or a symbol; He came Himself. The Lord of heaven chose to walk our roads, bear our sorrows, and share our joys. He came not to rule with power, but to rescue with mercy. Through Jesus, God did not remain distant from our pain — He entered into it, sanctified it, and transformed it.

This is the love we celebrate in Advent: a love that stoops low to lift us high, a love that chooses humility over majesty, and service over strength. The Word became flesh not only to save us from sin but to show us what true love looks like — love that sacrifices, love that forgives, love that never gives up.

When we gaze upon the manger, we are not just looking at a child; we are looking at **the heart of God revealed.** The infant wrapped in swaddling clothes is the same Word that holds the universe together. The hands that will one day bear the nails of Calvary are the same hands that now rest in Mary's gentle arms. The Incarnation is God's eternal "yes" to humanity — His promise that He will never abandon us.

To say that *"the Word became flesh"* is to say that God chose to speak to us not through commands or prophets alone, but through relationship. Jesus is God's love letter written in human form. Through Him, we can see, hear, and touch the love of the Father.

But this mystery also carries a challenge. If the Word became flesh, then we too must allow the Word to take flesh in us. God's love is not meant to remain an idea; it is meant to be lived. Every time we forgive, we make the Word flesh. Every time we serve, we make the Word flesh. Every time we love without condition, we make the Word flesh. Christ desires not only to dwell *among* us but *within* us — to speak through our voices, to act through our hands, and to shine through our hearts.

As Advent nears its fulfillment, let us pause in awe before this miracle of love. The same Word that spoke the universe into being now whispers to our hearts, calling us to make room for Him. The same Word that once lay in a manger now seeks to dwell within us.

Let us welcome Him — not as a distant God, but as Emmanuel, *God with us and God within us.*

Reflection:

The Word made flesh is the perfect revelation of God's love. Through Jesus, heaven and earth meet, eternity enters time, and divine love wears a human face.

Ask yourself: *Have I allowed the Word of God to take root in my heart? Do my words and actions reveal Christ to others?*

Advent reminds us that faith is not only about waiting for God to come — it is about recognizing that He is already here, living among us and within us.

Take time today to read the opening verses of John's Gospel (John 1:1–14). Let each word sink deeply into your heart. Listen for the voice of the Word that still speaks — in Scripture, in prayer, in silence, and in love.

Prayer:

Eternal Word,
You were with God in the beginning, and through You all things were made. Yet in Your infinite mercy, You chose to dwell among us — to take on our humanity so that we might share in Your divinity.

Thank You, Lord, for becoming flesh, for walking beside us, for speaking words of life, and for showing us the way of perfect love. As I prepare to celebrate Your birth, let my heart be open and ready to receive You anew.

Let Your Word take flesh in me, that I may speak with truth, love with compassion, and live with grace. May my life reflect Your light in a world still longing for hope.

Come, Lord Jesus — Word made flesh, dwell within me and make me an instrument of Your divine love.
Amen.

Saturday: The Eve of the Savior's Birth

Scripture Reading:

"For unto us a Child is born, unto us a Son is given; and the government shall be upon His shoulder; and His name shall be called Wonderful Counselor, Mighty God, Everlasting Father, Prince of Peace."
— **Isaiah 9:6**

The final candle glows in fullness now — the **Candle of Love** — and the circle of light on our Advent wreath is complete. The waiting is almost over. The long nights of longing give way to the dawn of divine promise. **It is the Eve of the Savior's Birth** — the holiest night before the holiest morning, when heaven bends low to kiss the earth, and the world holds its breath for the coming of the Christ Child.

There is a sacred hush that seems to fall upon creation on this night — a silence filled not with emptiness but with expectation. It is as though all of heaven and earth are holding still, waiting for the cry of a newborn King. This night bridges the promise and the fulfillment, the prophecy and the incarnation, the longing of humanity and the love of God made visible in flesh.

Advent has been a journey of hope, peace, joy, and love —
and all of it finds its completion here, in a manger in
Bethlehem. Every candle we have lit points to this moment.
Every prayer we have whispered finds its answer in the tiny
hands of the Infant Christ.

The night before Christ's birth is a night unlike any other. It
is the night when divine mystery unfolds in perfect
humility. The Savior of the world is about to enter not in
splendor or power, but in stillness and simplicity. The King
of kings chooses not a palace, but a stable. His first throne
will be a manger, His first attendants — humble shepherds.
Yet in this humility lies the greatest glory the world has
ever known.

The Eve of the Savior's Birth reminds us that love often
comes quietly. God's greatest works do not always arrive
with trumpets and crowds but in the stillness of surrender,
in the silence of faith, and in the gentle light of obedience.
Mary and Joseph, weary from their journey, settle in for the
night. The air is cool, the stars blaze above them, and deep
within Mary's heart, there is a peace that only love can
give.

This night calls us, too, to stillness — to quiet our hearts, to
prepare a manger within our souls where Christ may be
born anew. Amid the noise of our world, the rush of our
plans, and the weight of our worries, God still comes —
softly, faithfully, lovingly. His coming does not depend on
our perfection but on our openness.

The love that began in heaven will touch the earth tonight.
The Word that became flesh will soon cry out from the
arms of His mother. The same hands that shaped the stars
will soon reach out for human comfort. And with that first
breath, the world will never be the same again.

On this holy eve, we remember that Christmas is not merely a memory — it is a miracle that continues. Each time love is born in a human heart, each time forgiveness is offered, each time compassion triumphs over indifference, Christ is born again. The love that entered the world in Bethlehem continues to shine in those who believe.

Let this night be one of quiet adoration. Let it be a time to gaze with wonder at the mystery of love divine — a love that left the throne of heaven for the poverty of a stable, a love that became small so that we might be made great, a love that came to redeem and dwell within us forever.

As you light the final candle this night, let its flame remind you that Love Himself is coming — to dwell with us, to save us, to stay with us. Let your heart echo the words of the angels who will soon proclaim, *"Glory to God in the highest, and on earth peace to those on whom His favor rests."*

Reflection:

The Eve of the Savior's Birth is a sacred threshold between waiting and fulfillment, between faith and sight. Take time tonight to rest in the quiet wonder of God's plan — a plan fulfilled not through power, but through love.

Ask yourself: *Is my heart ready to receive the Christ Child? Have I made room for His love amid life's distractions?*

Let this night be your prayer — a night of stillness, gratitude, and awe. Kneel before the mystery of the manger, and let love be reborn within you.

Prayer:

Heavenly Father,
As the night deepens and the world waits, my heart turns to
You with wonder and gratitude. On this holy eve, I thank
You for the gift of Your Son — Love made flesh, the Light
that no darkness can overcome.

Prepare my heart to welcome Him anew. Quiet the noise
within me, still my restless thoughts, and make room for
Your peace. Let the joy of this night fill my soul, and let
Your love shine through me to others.

May I, like Mary and Joseph, bow in humble adoration
before the miracle of Your love.
Come, Lord Jesus — be born in me tonight. Dwell in my
heart, rule in my life, and fill the world once more with
Your saving grace.
Amen.

Part VI: The O Antiphons (December 17–23)

Introduction: The Ancient Prayer of Expectation

As Advent nears its fulfillment and the Church draws closer to the celebration of Christ's birth, the final days before Christmas are marked by a series of ancient and deeply moving prayers known as the **O Antiphons**.

Dating back to the early centuries of the Church, these short invocations — prayed from **December 17 to December 23** — express the longing of God's people for the coming of the Messiah. Each antiphon begins with the exclamation **"O"**, followed by a prophetic title of Christ drawn from Scripture — *O Wisdom, O Lord, O Root of Jesse, O Key of David, O Rising Sun, O King of Nations, O Emmanuel.*

The O Antiphons are like a sacred countdown, each one a candle of hope and expectation. They give voice to humanity's deepest yearning: that the Savior, long promised and long awaited, would come to dwell among us.

These prayers are not relics of the past; they are living words of faith that continue to prepare our hearts for the mystery of Christmas. As we pray them, we join the generations before us who have whispered the same ancient cry:

"Come, Lord Jesus!"

December 17 – O Wisdom (O Sapientia)

Antiphon:

"O Wisdom, who came forth from the mouth of the Most High,
reaching from end to end,
ordering all things mightily and sweetly:
come, and teach us the way of prudence."

As we begin the sacred journey of the **O Antiphons**, we first call upon **Christ, the Wisdom of God** — the eternal Word through whom all things were made. Before the stars were hung in the heavens or the mountains rose from the earth, He existed with the Father, perfect in knowledge, infinite in understanding, and boundless in love.

In Scripture, **Wisdom** is often portrayed as the guiding light of creation, the divine order behind all that is good and true. In the Book of Proverbs, she is described as one who was with God "before the beginning of His works" and who "rejoiced in His inhabited world and delighted in the sons of men" (Proverbs 8:22–31). This eternal Wisdom became flesh in Jesus Christ — the living revelation of God's perfect plan.

To call upon Christ as *O Wisdom* is to recognize our need for divine guidance in a world clouded by confusion and noise. It is to acknowledge that human understanding alone cannot lead us to true peace. We need the One who "reaches from end to end" — whose wisdom orders the universe and whose love sustains it — to teach us the way of holiness and prudence.

When we pray *O Wisdom*, we invite Christ to illuminate our minds and hearts, to bring harmony where there is disorder, clarity where there is uncertainty, and purpose where there is aimlessness. His wisdom does not humiliate or overpower; it gently directs and lovingly corrects. It teaches us not only what is right but how to live rightly.

Christ's wisdom is unlike the wisdom of the world. The world values cleverness, power, and success; Christ values humility, mercy, and love. His wisdom was revealed most clearly on the Cross — a paradox to human reason but the greatest truth of divine love. There, what seemed like defeat became victory; what appeared as weakness became strength.

As Advent draws near its fulfillment, we are called to seek this divine wisdom — to let Christ reorder our hearts according to His will. He desires to dwell not only in the grand halls of history but also in the quiet places of our souls, where His gentle wisdom can take root.

Reflection:

Take a few moments today to sit in silence before the Lord and ask for the gift of wisdom. Where are you in need of divine understanding? Is there a decision, a burden, or a relationship that needs the light of Christ's truth?

Pray that His wisdom may not only enlighten your mind but transform your heart — that you may see life not merely as it is, but as God sees it.

Prayer:

O Wisdom of God Most High,
You order all things with power and love.
Come into my heart and guide me in Your truth.
Teach me to discern Your will and to walk in Your ways with peace and understanding.

Dispel the darkness of confusion and pride,
and fill me with the light of Your divine counsel.
Let Your wisdom dwell in me,
that my thoughts, words, and actions may reflect Your eternal plan of love.

Come, O Wisdom,
and make me wise in the ways of Your Kingdom.
Amen.

December 18 – O Adonai (O Lord of Might)

Antiphon:

"O Adonai, and Leader of the house of Israel,
You appeared to Moses in the flame of the burning bush,
and gave him the law on Mount Sinai:
come and redeem us with an outstretched arm."

On this second evening of the **O Antiphons**, the Church calls upon Christ as **O Adonai** — the Hebrew name meaning *Lord*, the same sacred title by which God revealed Himself to His people in the Old Testament. In this prayer, we acknowledge Jesus not only as our Redeemer but as the eternal Lord who has guided, protected, and delivered His people from age to age.

To call Christ *Adonai* is to recognize that the Child soon to be born in Bethlehem is the same God who spoke to Moses from the burning bush, saying, *"I AM WHO AM"* (Exodus 3:14). The same divine voice that thundered on Mount Sinai now whispers in the quiet cry of a newborn Child. The Lord of power and majesty comes to us not in fire and smoke, but in gentleness and humility.

When we pray *O Adonai*, we remember that the God who once delivered Israel from bondage in Egypt now delivers us from the slavery of sin. His arm is still mighty to save; His mercy still reaches out to rescue. He is both the Lawgiver and the Redeemer — the One who commands righteousness and the One who gives grace to fulfill it.

The burning bush that blazed without being consumed is a symbol of divine mystery — a foreshadowing of the Incarnation. Just as the bush burned but was not destroyed, so Mary bore the divine fire of God's presence within her womb and remained pure. In her, heaven and earth met; the uncreated Word took on created flesh. Through her obedience, *Adonai* entered the world as Emmanuel, *God with us*.

Christ as *Adonai* is both majesty and mercy. He holds the law in one hand and the cross in the other. He commands holiness, yet bends low to lift us when we fall. He is the same Lord who stretches out His hand — not in judgment, but in salvation.

As Advent nears its end, we are invited to reflect on this great paradox: the Lord of Might comes as a helpless infant; the One who rules the universe humbles Himself to serve. This is the mystery of love — power wrapped in meekness, majesty clothed in mercy.

When we cry out *"Come, O Adonai!"* we are not only calling for God to act in history but to act within us — to free us from all that binds us, to write His law of love upon our hearts, and to rule not by force but by grace.

Reflection:

Reflect today on the Lordship of Christ in your life. Is He truly *Adonai* — the One who reigns in your heart and directs your steps?

Consider the areas where you still resist His guidance or try to rely on your own strength. Ask Him to redeem those places with His mighty arm and to bring freedom where there is fear, and obedience where there is hesitation.

Remember: the God who revealed Himself in fire now reveals Himself in love. Let His light burn brightly within you.

Prayer:

O Adonai, Lord of Might,
You appeared to Moses in the burning bush
and gave Your people the law of life on Mount Sinai.
Now You come to us in the humility of the manger —
the same eternal Word made flesh for our salvation.

Stretch out Your mighty arm and redeem us, O Lord.
Free us from the slavery of sin and the chains of selfishness.
Write Your law of love upon our hearts,
that we may walk in Your truth and live as Your faithful people.

Come, O Adonai,
and rule with justice, mercy, and peace.
Make my heart a dwelling place for Your presence,

and teach me to serve You with joy and obedience.
Amen.

December 19 – O Root of Jesse (O Radix Jesse)

Antiphon:

"O Root of Jesse, who stands as a sign to the peoples;
before whom kings shall shut their mouths,
to whom the nations shall make their prayer:
come and deliver us, and delay no longer."

On this third evening of the **O Antiphons**, our prayer rises like incense toward the One called **O Root of Jesse** — the promised shoot springing forth from the ancient line of King David. This image, drawn from Isaiah's prophecy (*Isaiah 11:1–10*), speaks of the hope that grows even from what seems lifeless:
"A shoot shall come out from the stump of Jesse, and from his roots a Branch shall bear fruit."

In the days of Isaiah, Israel's royal line — descended from Jesse, the father of David — had been cut down by sin, exile, and despair. What once stood tall like a mighty tree now appeared as a dead stump. Yet the prophet saw what human eyes could not: from that stump, God would bring forth new life. The Messiah would rise from this humble root, and His kingdom would be one of righteousness, peace, and everlasting love.

When we call upon Christ as *O Root of Jesse*, we proclaim Him as the fulfillment of that promise — the One who brings life from death, hope from ruin, and renewal from desolation. The world had grown weary and dry from sin, but in the fullness of time, new life broke forth in Bethlehem. From Mary's womb, like a tender shoot, sprang the Savior — the living proof that God's promises never die.

The title "Root of Jesse" reminds us that God's work is often hidden, slow, and surprising. What seems dead to us is never beyond His power to revive. Like roots buried deep in the soil, God's grace works quietly beneath the surface, preparing the way for new growth. Even when we cannot see it, His plan is unfolding.

This antiphon also reminds us that Christ is not only Israel's hope but the hope of **all nations**. He is the sign to which every heart turns and the fulfillment of every longing. Before Him, kings fall silent; in Him, the restless find peace. The Root of Jesse has grown into a Tree of Life, whose branches reach to every corner of the world.

In our own lives, there are times when faith feels like that old, withered stump — when joy seems distant, and hope feels fragile. Yet Advent assures us that God can bring life even there. If we open our hearts, the Root of Jesse can plant new beginnings within us, restoring what has been broken and reviving what has been lost.

Reflection:

Where in your life do you feel something has been "cut down" or lost? Is there an area that seems beyond renewal — a dream, a relationship, or a hope that feels withered?

Invite Christ, the Root of Jesse, to breathe life into that place. Trust that His grace is already at work, quietly restoring and strengthening you.

The God who brought a Savior from a dead stump can bring healing and fruitfulness from even the most barren ground of your soul.

Prayer:

O Root of Jesse,
You spring forth as a sign of hope for all the nations.
From the stump of human weakness,
You bring forth new life that never fades.

Come, Lord Jesus,
and take root in my heart.
Revive the places in me that feel dry or broken.
Let Your mercy restore what sin has wounded,
and let Your grace bear fruit in my life once more.

May Your Kingdom of peace and justice flourish in me and throughout the world.
Come quickly, O Root of Jesse —
do not delay in bringing Your new life to all creation.
Amen.

December 20 – O Key of David
(O Clavis David)

Antiphon:

"O Key of David and Scepter of the House of Israel,
You open and no one can shut;
You shut and no one can open:
come and lead the prisoners from the prison house,
those who dwell in darkness and the shadow of death."

On this fourth evening of the **O Antiphons**, the Church calls upon Christ as the **Key of David** — *O Clavis David* — the One who unlocks what no one else can open, and who closes what no one else can shut. This image, rich in meaning, is drawn from **Isaiah 22:22**, where the prophet foretells a ruler to whom God will entrust the key of the house of David, giving him authority to open and close as He wills.

This prophecy finds its fulfillment in Christ, the true Son of David, who holds the keys not only to the kingdom of Israel but to the Kingdom of Heaven itself. *"I have the keys of death and of Hades,"* He declares in Revelation 1:18. He alone has the power to open the gates of salvation, to release those held captive by sin, and to bring light to those who sit in darkness.

To call Jesus the *Key of David* is to recognize Him as the door through which humanity is restored to God. What Adam's disobedience closed, Christ's obedience has opened. By His cross and resurrection, the locked gate of Paradise has been thrown wide. The chains of sin and death have been broken forever, and the way to eternal life stands open for all who believe.

When we pray *O Clavis David*, we are asking Christ to open the doors of our hearts — to free us from whatever keeps us imprisoned within ourselves. It is a plea for liberation from guilt, fear, pride, resentment, or despair. Only He can unlock these inner prisons and set us free to walk in the light of His mercy.

There are doors in every life that only Christ can open. Some lead to healing; others, to forgiveness. Some are the doors of reconciliation, long closed by hurt or misunderstanding. Some are the doors of courage, through which we must pass to follow God's call. Jesus holds the key to them all. When we allow Him to turn that key within us, grace flows freely, peace returns, and love is restored.

The *Key of David* is also the scepter of divine authority. Christ reigns not as a distant ruler but as a merciful Lord who governs with compassion. His authority does not enslave; it liberates. His rule is not one of fear but of freedom — the freedom of the children of God.

The One who opens the gates of heaven also opens the secret chambers of our hearts. He knows our struggles, our hidden wounds, and our deepest longings. His love is the master key that fits every lock. And when He opens our hearts, His light floods in, dispelling every shadow of sin and sorrow.

Reflection:

What are the locked doors in your life? Is there a part of
your heart that you have kept closed — out of fear, regret,
or pain?

Invite Christ, the Key of David, to enter those places. Let
Him unlock what is bound, heal what is wounded, and free
what is captive. Trust that the One who opened the tomb
will open the way to new life for you.

Remember: no door is too tightly shut, no heart too
hardened, no sin too deep for the Key of David to redeem.

Prayer:

O Key of David,
You open the gates of heaven and free those imprisoned by
sin.
Unlock the doors of my heart and release me from
everything that binds me.

Break the chains of fear and pride that keep me from loving
You fully.
Open the paths of peace and grace within my life.
May Your mercy flow freely through me, bringing healing
to every place in need of Your touch.

Come, Lord Jesus — Key of David and Prince of Freedom.
Open for me the door of salvation, and guide me into the
light of Your eternal love.
Amen.

December 21 – O Dayspring (O Oriens)

Antiphon:

"O Dayspring, Splendor of Eternal Light and Sun of Justice,
come and shine on those who dwell in darkness
and the shadow of death."

As the final days of Advent draw us closer to Christmas, tonight we lift our hearts in prayer to **Christ, our Dayspring** — *O Oriens* — the Rising Sun who breaks through the night and fills the world with light.

This beautiful antiphon captures one of the most beloved images of Christ in all of Scripture: light dawning upon darkness. The prophets foretold it centuries before His birth — *"The people who walked in darkness have seen a great light; upon those who lived in a land of deep darkness, a light has shone."* (Isaiah 9:2).

That light is Jesus — the eternal Sun of Justice who rises not in the sky, but in the human heart. His coming scatters fear, heals sin, and brings warmth to the cold and weary soul. He is the new dawn after the long night of sin; the Light that cannot be overcome.

When we call Him *Dayspring*, we are naming Him as the source of all renewal — the One who makes all things new. He is the beginning of every good thing, the end of all darkness, the hope that rises after despair. His light does not merely illuminate our path; it transforms our vision, helping us to see the world and one another through the eyes of love.

The image of the rising sun also reminds us that God's mercy is faithful and constant. Just as dawn follows every night without fail, so His grace rises upon us again and again. No matter how long the night of our sorrow or struggle may seem, the Light of Christ is never far away. His coming is sure.

In our spiritual lives, we sometimes find ourselves walking through darkness — the darkness of uncertainty, grief, temptation, or loneliness. But it is precisely into that darkness that the Dayspring shines most brightly. The love of Christ reaches even into the deepest shadows to bring peace and healing.

The sun does not rush when it rises; it ascends gently, spreading light little by little until the whole world glows. So too does Christ's grace often work in quiet, gradual ways — softening hearts, restoring faith, and awakening joy. His light is patient and kind.

As we near Christmas, we are called not only to rejoice in His coming light but to *reflect* it. Those who live in Christ become bearers of His brightness to others. Our words, our kindness, our mercy — these become the rays of His rising that reach into the dark corners of the world.

Reflection:

Where do you need the light of Christ to shine in your life today? Is there an area overshadowed by worry, guilt, or sorrow?

Invite the Dayspring to rise there. Ask Him to dispel the darkness with His presence and to warm your heart with His peace.

And then, consider how you can carry that light to others — to someone lonely, discouraged, or forgotten. The light you share may be the very dawn another soul has been praying for.

Prayer:

O Dayspring,
Radiant Light of the Eternal Father,
You shine upon those who dwell in darkness and bring hope to the shadowed heart.

Come, Lord Jesus, and light my way.
Dispel the darkness of fear and doubt within me.
Let the warmth of Your love heal the coldness of my soul.
Rise upon me like the morning sun, and fill my life with the brightness of Your grace.

Help me to reflect Your light to others,
that through my words and deeds,
the world may see the glory of Your love.

Come, O Dayspring, Sun of Justice —
shine upon the nations and upon every heart that waits for
You.
Amen.

December 22 – O King of the Nations (O Rex Gentium)

Antiphon:

"O King of the Nations, and their Desire,
the Cornerstone who makes both one:
come and save mankind,
whom You formed from the dust of the earth."

As the final candles of Advent flicker toward Christmas, tonight the Church lifts her voice in praise to **Christ our King** — *O Rex Gentium*, the **King of the Nations** and the **Cornerstone** of unity and peace.

This ancient title gathers the hopes of the world into one single, royal plea: *"Come and save mankind."* From the beginning of time, God has been shaping the story of humanity — a story that began with His own hands forming us from the dust of the earth. Though sin divided and scattered us, the love of Christ, our King, comes to restore what was lost, to gather what was broken, and to reign in every heart that welcomes Him.

The prophets long foretold this universal King. Isaiah proclaimed, *"He shall judge between the nations and shall decide for many peoples; they shall beat their swords into plowshares, and their spears into pruning hooks."* (Isaiah 2:4). In Him, division gives way to harmony, and hatred is transformed into peace.

When we call Christ the *King of the Nations*, we confess that His dominion knows no boundary — not of race, language, or land. His kingdom is not one of power and conquest but of **love, justice, and mercy**. He reigns not from a throne of gold but from the wood of the Cross. There, the true measure of kingship is revealed: not domination, but self-giving love.

The antiphon also calls Him the **Cornerstone**, echoing the words of the psalmist: *"The stone that the builders rejected has become the cornerstone."* (Psalm 118:22). Christ unites all peoples — Jew and Gentile, rich and poor, strong and weak — into one spiritual house, one holy family. Without Him as the foundation, the structure of our lives cannot stand.

In a world fractured by conflict and divided by pride, we need the reign of this King more than ever. His rule brings reconciliation; His peace surpasses understanding. When we allow Him to reign in our hearts, He begins to build His kingdom there — a kingdom of compassion, truth, and mercy that spreads outward to the world.

To pray *O Rex Gentium* is to invite Christ to rule over our thoughts, our relationships, and our choices. It is to say, "Be my King — not just in name, but in every part of my life." And when we do, His love begins to bring order where there was confusion, peace where there was turmoil, and unity where there was division.

On this eve before the final antiphon, our prayer deepens into longing: *Come, Lord Jesus — unite Your scattered children and reign over all creation with love.*

Reflection:

Is Christ truly King in your life? Does His love govern your thoughts, your words, and your actions?

Ask Him to reign in your heart completely — to bring peace where there is conflict, unity where there is division, and faith where there is fear.

Remember: every time you choose love over anger, forgiveness over bitterness, or peace over pride, you proclaim His kingship. Let Him be the cornerstone of your home, your relationships, your faith, and your future.

Prayer:

O King of the Nations,
Long-awaited Desire of every human heart,
You unite all people in Yourself and make us one family of grace.
Come and reign in my heart,
that Your peace may rule where conflict has reigned,
and Your love may bind what sin has divided.

You are the Cornerstone of the world's salvation.
Build in me a dwelling place for Your glory.
Make me an instrument of reconciliation and a witness to Your kingdom of peace.

Come, Lord Jesus, King of the Nations —
gather the peoples of the earth beneath Your gentle reign,
and teach us to live as one in the love of the Father.
Amen.

December 23 – O Emmanuel (God With Us)

Antiphon:

*"O Emmanuel, our King and Lawgiver,
the Desire of the Nations and their Savior:
come and save us, O Lord our God."*

The final evening of the **O Antiphons** has arrived, and the Church's ancient prayer reaches its tender climax with the most beautiful name of all — **O Emmanuel**, meaning **"God with us."**

This title, spoken by the prophet Isaiah (*Isaiah 7:14*), captures the entire mystery of Advent and the heart of the Gospel itself. For weeks we have cried, *"Come!"* — come, O Wisdom; come, O Lord; come, O Root of Jesse; come, O Key of David; come, O Rising Sun; come, O King. And now, in this final invocation, the Church's longing becomes fulfillment: **He has come — God Himself is with us.**

O Emmanuel is not only a name; it is a promise — the promise that the Creator of the universe has not remained distant, but has entered into our humanity to dwell among us. The infinite became finite, the invisible became visible, and the eternal Word took on mortal flesh. The One who made the stars was born beneath them.

When we speak the name Emmanuel, we remember that God's love is not abstract or far away; it is **personal, present, and near.** He does not stand apart from our suffering but shares it. He does not watch from a distance but walks beside us. He is not merely "God above us" or "God beyond us," but **God with us** — in our joy, our pain, our weakness, and our hope.

In Jesus Christ, every longing heart finds its rest. The Desire of all nations has come to gather His people into one family of love. The Savior we awaited is not only a King to rule us, but a Brother to walk with us. His presence transforms everything — fear into peace, sorrow into joy, death into life.

This final antiphon brings the Advent journey full circle. All that we have prayed and waited for now finds its fulfillment in the Word made flesh. Emmanuel is the answer to every cry of the human soul. He is the wisdom we seek, the freedom we long for, the light we need, and the love that redeems.

As we stand at the threshold of Christmas, the prayer *"Come, Lord Jesus"* becomes an invitation not only for the birth we commemorate but for the continual coming of Christ into our lives. He is Emmanuel every day — in the Eucharist, in His Word, in the poor and the suffering, and in the quiet stirrings of our hearts.

So tonight, as the last candle of Advent burns low, we rest in the stillness of expectation — knowing that the dawn is near, that the Child of promise is coming, and that Love Himself will soon be born among us.

Reflection:

Pause for a few moments of silence and whisper His name: **Emmanuel**.

Let that holy name sink deeply into your soul. Where in your life do you need to feel that God is truly *with you*? In your family? In your work? In your struggles? In your waiting?

Invite Him there. He desires not only to visit but to dwell — to make His home within your heart. Let your soul become Bethlehem, a place where Love may be born anew.

Prayer:

O Emmanuel,
God with us,
You are the Light in our darkness,
the Hope of our hearts,
and the Joy of every longing soul.

Come, dwell among us,
and fill our lives with Your presence.
Be near to those who suffer,
comfort the lonely,
and bring peace to a weary world.

Lord Jesus, You are the fulfillment of every promise,
the answer to every prayer,
and the gift beyond all gifts.
Come and reign in our hearts now and forever.

O Emmanuel, our King and our Savior —
be born anew in us this night.
Amen.

Christmas Eve: The Christ Candle – The Light of the World Has Come

Scripture Reading:

The Birth of Jesus — Luke 2:1–20

"And she gave birth to her firstborn son and wrapped him in swaddling cloths and laid him in a manger, because there was no room for them in the inn. And in that region there were shepherds out in the field, keeping watch over their flock by night. And an angel of the Lord appeared to them, and the glory of the Lord shone around them, and they were filled with great fear. But the angel said to them, 'Do not be afraid; for behold, I bring you good news of great joy that will be for all the people. For unto you is born this day in the city of David a Savior, who is Christ the Lord.'"

Reflection: Light for All Nations

At last, the long-awaited night has come. The waiting, the
longing, the prayer, and the hope of generations all find
their fulfillment in this sacred moment: **the Light of the
World has come.**

On this holy night, the final candle — the **Christ Candle**
— is lit at the center of the Advent wreath. Its pure, radiant
flame symbolizes Jesus Christ, the true Light that no
darkness can overcome. It stands as the heart of all the
other candles — for hope, peace, joy, and love all find their
meaning in Him. Every flicker of light we have kindled
through Advent has led to this brilliant illumination: the
birth of the Savior.

In the stillness of the Bethlehem night, the world changed
forever. Heaven touched earth, eternity entered time, and
the Word became flesh. God did not come as a warrior or a
ruler, but as a Child — small, vulnerable, and wrapped in
swaddling cloths. The glory of God was veiled in
simplicity, and the majesty of heaven was laid in a manger.

The angels sang; the shepherds rejoiced; the heavens burst
with praise. For the Light had entered the darkness, and the
darkness could not overcome it.

This is more than a story of the past — it is a living truth
for every generation. The same Christ who was born in
Bethlehem desires to be born again in every believing
heart. His light still shines in the darkness of our world —

in every act of mercy, every word of kindness, every heart that chooses love over fear.

When we light the Christ Candle, we proclaim that the waiting is over — Emmanuel, *God with us*, has come. The One foretold by prophets and awaited by the faithful through centuries is here. The promise has been fulfilled; salvation has dawned.

Yet the message of Christmas does not end with wonder — it calls us to mission. The Light that entered the world is not meant to be kept to ourselves. Like the shepherds who ran to tell the good news, we too are called to bear witness to the light we have seen. The joy of this night is meant to be shared — in our homes, our communities, and our world.

And so, as the flame of the Christ Candle glows brightly in our midst, it reminds us that **Christ is not only the Light of the world — He is the Light of our lives.** His love dispels the shadows of fear, His truth pierces through the lies of despair, and His mercy renews every weary soul.

Tonight, as you gaze upon that candle's steady glow, let its light draw you into prayerful stillness. Let it remind you that even when life feels dark, the Light of Christ still burns brightly — guiding, comforting, and redeeming.

He is the dawn that never fades, the promise that never fails, the love that never ends.

Prayer: Welcoming Christ into Our Hearts

Lord Jesus Christ,
On this holy night, I welcome You with joy and awe. You
are the Light of the world, shining into the darkness of
every heart and every nation. You have come — not in
grandeur, but in humility; not in might, but in mercy.

I thank You for the gift of Your presence — for the love
that became flesh and dwelt among us. As the shepherds
came in haste to adore You, I, too, come in faith and
gratitude. I bring You my heart — poor and simple — and
ask You to make it Your home.

Light of the world, shine in me.
Dispel the shadows of sin and fear.
Let Your peace fill my soul, and Your love flow through
me to others.
As I kneel at the manger, I offer You my praise, my trust,
and my life.

Come, Lord Jesus — dwell in me tonight.
Let Your light burn brightly in my heart, that I may carry it
into the world.
May my words, my actions, and my love reflect Your
glory,
and may the joy of Your birth fill the earth with hope.

Amen.

Christmas Day: A Prayer of Celebration

Scripture Reading:

"And suddenly there was with the angel a multitude of the heavenly host praising God and saying,
'Glory to God in the highest, and on earth peace, good will toward men.'"
— **Luke 2:13–14**

Reflection: The Joy of Christ's Birth

The dawn has come at last. The waiting of Advent is over, and the world rejoices with holy gladness — **Christ the Savior is born!**

The Light we have longed for through the weeks of preparation now shines in all its brilliance. Heaven and earth unite in song, and the words of the angels echo through every heart that believes: *"Glory to God in the highest!"*

On this sacred morning, love has triumphed, peace has descended, and hope has taken human form. The Lord of all creation, the Word through whom the universe was made, has come to dwell among us — not as a mighty ruler, but as a humble Child. The infinite God became small, the eternal entered time, and the Creator became one with His creation.

In the manger, we behold the mystery of divine love — a love so boundless that it stooped low to meet us in our need. The same God who holds the galaxies in His hands now rests in the arms of Mary. The same voice that thundered at Sinai now coos softly in Bethlehem. The One who sustains all life now depends on the care of His creatures. This is the miracle and the humility of Christmas: **God with us — Emmanuel.**

Today, all creation rejoices, for the promise made long ago has been fulfilled. The light of the prophets, the hope of the poor, the joy of the faithful — all have found their answer in this Child. The heavens proclaim His glory, the shepherds adore Him, and we, too, are called to kneel before His majesty in simplicity and wonder.

Christmas is not just a remembrance; it is a renewal. The same Christ who was born in Bethlehem longs to be born again in every human heart. His coming is not confined to history — it is an ever-present invitation. Each Christmas, He knocks anew at the door of our souls, waiting for our response. Will we open our hearts as the stable opened its doors? Will we welcome Him into the humble places of our lives, where His grace can shine most brightly?

The joy of this day is meant to overflow — to be carried from the manger into the world. Like the shepherds who "made known what had been told them concerning this Child," we are called to bear witness to the love we have seen. Christmas joy is not complete until it is shared. Every act of kindness, every word of peace, every gift of compassion becomes a continuation of that first holy night's message: *"Glory to God in the highest, and on earth peace."*

So let us rejoice — not only with our voices, but with our lives. Let our hearts sing with gratitude for the gift of salvation. Let our homes reflect the warmth of God's love, and let our lives shine with the light of His presence.

On this day, heaven touches earth once more. The Savior has come, and the world will never be the same.

Prayer: A Prayer of Celebration

O Holy and Merciful God,
Today my heart overflows with joy and gratitude.
You have fulfilled Your promise — You have come to dwell among us.
The light of the world shines brightly,
and the darkness has been scattered by Your glory.

Lord Jesus Christ,
I praise You for the wonder of Your birth,
for the humility of the manger,
and for the love that moved You to become one of us.
You are my hope, my peace, my joy, and my salvation.

As the angels sang, *"Glory to God in the highest,"*
so now I lift my voice in praise to You.
May all the earth rejoice in Your coming.
Let every heart be opened, every soul renewed, every life transformed by Your grace.

Bless, O Lord, this holy day.
Fill our homes with laughter, our tables with thanksgiving,
and our hearts with Your peace.
Let the love born in Bethlehem shine through me
to everyone I meet,
so that the world may see in my life the reflection of Your
light.

Come, Lord Jesus — dwell always within me.
Rule my heart as King, guide my steps as Shepherd,
and fill me with the joy of Your presence, now and forever.

Amen.

Printed in Dunstable, United Kingdom